**INSIGHT POCKET GUIDE**

Kuala Lumpur

Discovery CHANNEL

APA PUBLICATIONS
Part of the Langenscheidt Publishing Group

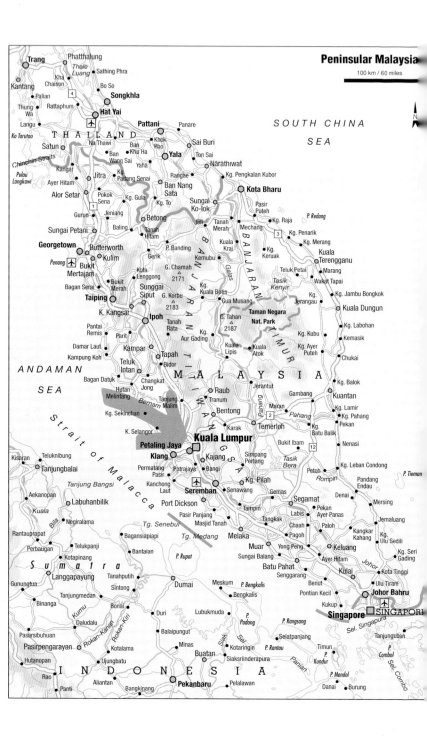

Peninsular Malaysia

100 km / 60 miles

introduction

Welcome

This guidebook combines the interests and enthusiasms of two of the world's best-known information providers: Insight Guides, who have set the standard for visual travel guides since 1970, and Discovery Channel, the world's premier source of non-fiction television programming. Its aim is to bring you the best of Kuala Lumpur city and its surroundings in a series of tailor-made itineraries devised by Insight's Malaysia-based correspondent, SL Wong.

The capital of Malaysia, Kuala Lumpur was a run-down shanty town on the edge of a marshy riverbank some 150 years ago. Today, this former mining outpost has transformed itself into a burgeoning multicultural city of two million, with a skyline that boasts the tallest buildings in the world. The first three full-day itineraries string together the most essential sights of KL (as its inhabitants fondly refer to it), from the historic heart of the city to Chinatown and the leafy Lake Gardens.

These are followed by a series of optional tours which cover sights as diverse as Kampung Bahru – KL's Malay quarter, the Hindu cave temple at Batu Caves, and the bustling mega-malls of Bukit Bintang. For visitors with more time, there are excursions to remote islands and highland resorts. Chapters on shopping, eating out and nightlife, plus a practical information section covering travel essentials complete this reader-friendly guide.

 SL Wong is a Malaysia-born freelance writer who has used Kuala Lumpur as her base for well over a decade. Having worked and lived in Australia, Singapore and Hong Kong, she is proud to be a part of the city's eclectic blend of Asian chaos and Western-style modernity. KL is a city shaped in startling ways by its multifarious cultures, and by both old and new world influences. Yet it is grounded in the earthiness of inherited traditions and by the ethnicity of its people.

For both work and play, during the day and at night, Wong finds that the city offers so much in its quiet spaces and frenzied urbanity, matched by delicious food and friendly people. And only a short drive away are the calm and charm of rustic island life and the peace of tropical greenery.

This edition owes its foundations to the original edition written by Shoba Devan.

contents

Pages 2/3: the Moorish-inspired Sultan Abdul Samad Building **Following** Pages 8/9: festive National Day Parade

History & Culture

history/culture

Kuala Lumpur was never the centre of an ancient culture or civilisation. No philosopher, scientist or general can lay claim to its inspiration. Indeed, just 150 years ago, it was nothing more than marsh, muck and mudbank.

In 1857, an expedition of Chinese tin miners headed up the Klang River from Pengkalan Batu (now Port Klang), then the capital of the Sultanate of Selangor in Malaya. They were prospecting for tin, a mineral that commanded the kind of attention that is reserved for oil these days. After several days, they arrived at the confluence of the Klang and Gombak rivers, where they had to stop as the rivers were too shallow to accommodate their fully-laden flotilla. Their resting place was nothing more than a tiny hamlet nestled in a quagmire of mud. Appropriately, the miners called the place Kuala Lumpur – literally meaning 'muddy confluence'.

Tin was eventually found in Ampang, upstream of Kuala Lumpur, but because the rivers were shallow, direct access to the mines was limited. Thus, Kuala Lumpur became a convenient staging point for supplies and ore to be brought in or sent out. Buoyed by high tin prices, Kuala Lumpur developed into a flourishing village by the 1860s. Chinese labourers were imported by the thousands to operate the mines that had opened up its hinterland. There were some Malays – mainly Bugis traders from Celebes – but the Chinese immigrants began to dominate. Soon, Kuala Lumpur took on the veneer of a booming mining town – with seedy brothels, gambling dens and organised crime.

Self-Governance

The aristocrats of Selangor at first did not interfere with this development. They were content to collect export duties from the mined ore, and left the control of the Chinese

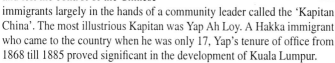

immigrants largely in the hands of a community leader called the 'Kapitan China'. The most illustrious Kapitan was Yap Ah Loy. A Hakka immigrant who came to the country when he was only 17, Yap's tenure of office from 1868 till 1885 proved significant in the development of Kuala Lumpur.

Gradually, Kuala Lumpur grew in prominence. In 1867, Selangor was torn by civil war; the bone of contention being the right to collect export duties on tin. Initially, the war focused on gaining control of the forts sited at the river estuaries where the Malay royalty was based. The miners of Kuala Lumpur, fearing the war, shipped their ore through whatever river route was open to them. However, as duties from tin slowly dwindled in the ports, the warring parties moved into Kuala Lumpur.

Left: 19th-century street scene in Kuala Lumpur
Right: a Malayan *prahu* (boat) dating back to the 1880s

Meanwhile, Yap Ah Loy allied himself with Tengku Kudin, the Viceroy of Selangor. His enemies were led by Syed Hashor, a determined and resourceful man who enlisted the help of other Malay chiefs and overran Kuala Lumpur in August 1872, razing it to the ground. However, in 1873, Tengku Kudin, with the help of Malay forces from Pahang, regained the town.

Yap Ah Loy is credited with ensuring that Kuala Lumpur did not disappear back into the marsh. After the war, with the town ruined and tin prices low, the Chinese immigrants were ready to pack up and leave. Yap, however, borrowed capital to redevelop Kuala Lumpur and cajoled the immigrants into staying to inspire confidence. Five years later, the strategy paid off as tin prices soared. In 1879, for the first time, a British official was stationed in Kuala Lumpur and in 1880, Selangor moved its capital to Kuala Lumpur.

The City's Resurrection

The next major personality in the city's history was Frank Swettenham, the Resident of Selangor appointed in 1882. Swettenham replaced the shanties and huts that formed much of Kuala Lumpur with brick structures. He was also responsible for the construction of the Kuala Lumpur–Klang railway link, ending the city's dependence on the river.

The city continued to grow. An active policy of emigration, the setting aside of reserves, and the encouragement of agriculture on its periphery increased the Malay population while diminishing the economic stronghold of the Chinese migrants. Indian labourers were brought in to work on coffee and rubber estates and on the railroad. The city became more cosmopolitan.

In 1896, Kuala Lumpur was declared the capital of the Federated Malay States. Both world wars did little damage to the city, and in 1957, 100 years

after the first mining expedition, the campsite was finally deemed worthy as the capital of sovereign Malaya. In 1963, Kuala Lumpur became the capital of Malaysia, and in 1972, it gained city status. Significantly, the city was also wrenched from Selangor and declared a Federal Territory in 1974, similar to the status enjoyed by Washington's District of Columbia. Since then the city has bloomed into one of the fastest growing in Southeast Asia. However, in some areas, basic infrastructure has not kept pace with the city's unbridled growth. The traffic jams, pollution and crowded streets are evidence of this.

World-Class Capital

In recent years, KL, as the city is known, has been erecting massive new buildings as a symbol of its aspirations to be a proud capital, not merely of Malaysia, but the world. These skyscrapers are seen as embodiments of the country's aim to be the spokesperson of Southeast Asia in global dialogues from trade and finance to information technology and international security. These and other national mega-projects, a good selection of which are found in the capital, are funded largely by foreign borrowings, something which has not been overly helpful to the country's debt levels.

KL's impressive skyline and its modern structures do give it the feel of an international city. Some visitors like this, since they can find enough global stamps of familiarity to be able to take to the city easily. From fast-food outlets and hotel chains to shopping malls and department stores, international brand names and products abound, at least superficially so; occasionally, some aspects are tempered with local quirkiness, such as Indian curry pizzas and four-star accommodation without the requisite 24-hour room service.

On the other hand, visitors expecting an ancient city untainted by Western norms, and with traditional architectural heritage intact, are likely to be disappointed with the modernity of KL. There are, however, pockets of the old KL – the ones that every city, no matter how modern, still possesses. So you might come across a colourful Hindu temple at a busy junction, or a row of pre-war shophouses behind a mall, while the sound of squawking chickens could well lead you to a wet market that has existed for generations. However, these finds might serve only to reinforce how rapidly the erosion of unique traditions has occurred, and will continue to occur, as KL and Malaysia seek to find a foothold in an era of globalisation.

Luckily, the city's more contemporary structures of glass and steel conveniently appeal to enough camera-happy visitors to make tourism one of the city's biggest revenue-earners. In fact, buildings like Petronas Twin Towers – the world's tallest buildings currently – are gradually taking precedence over the traditional tourism attractions that date back to colonial times.

Top left: Frank Swettenham, the Resident of Selangor
Left: most early Chinese migrants worked as labourers
Right: Kuala Lumpur's Petronas Twin Towers

A Melting Pot

Visitors to Kuala Lumpur will be fascinated by its obvious multi-culturalism: predominantly Malays, with smaller groups of Chinese, Indians, Eurasians, Portuguese and many people of mixed races. At one time, the city was divided along racial lines, with members of a race dominating an entire neighbourhood. These days, racially diverse neighbourhoods are more common.

Still, certain areas remain the stronghold of one dominant race. The Chinese occupy Chinatown of course, and much of the nearby Pudu, Sungai Besi and Salak South areas. They are mainly Cantonese, though a fair number of Hokkiens live there as well. Most of the Chinese population are adherents of the traditional Taoist and Buddhist faiths, though a substantial number have adopted Christianity.

The Malays have tended to congregate in the Kampung Bahru, Datuk Keramat, Ulu Kelang, Ampang and Sungai Pencala areas. Many still have *kampung* or village roots outside the city, but this is slowly changing. All are Muslims (to renounce Islam is a crime punishable by the law), hence the profusion of mosques, particularly in Malay neighbourhoods. However, liberalism is practised, and tolerance towards other religions has grown beyond mere lip service to the constitutional right to freedom of faith for other races. This is physically manifested in the presence of places of worship of other religious denominations, even in the capital's Malay heart of Kampung Bahru.

The Indian neighbourhoods are mainly in the Jalan Tun Sambanthan and Sentul areas. Their presence here is related to the fact that Malayan Railways once maintained housing for their labourers in these areas. Most of the Indians were originally from South India, but a fair sprinkling of Northerners – notably Punjabis, Sindhis and Gujeratis – also came to Kuala Lumpur for business. Sri Lankan Tamils were also brought over by the colonial authorities as administrative and clerical staff. Indians are mainly Hindu, though there is a very prominent Indian-Muslim community in Kuala Lumpur.

Nonetheless, racial harmony is very much in evidence. Chinese and Malay businessmen in shirt sleeves and ties sweat out a curry lunch at an Indian restaurant. Uniform jeans-and-T-shirt-clad youth of indeterminate racial origin hang out at the malls. Weekends find nightclubs filled with slinkily-dressed, trendy 20- and 30-somethings, gyrating to American R&B or Chilean Latin grooves, even while some in the group might abstain from alcohol or beef for religious purposes. And at the annual City Day Big Walk, people from all backgrounds turn out in their track suits or shorts to put their best leg forward for health and a good cause.

The kaleidoscopic nature of Kuala Lumpur society has given rise to a host of social and religious norms, some of which apply to only one community and others to all. It is traditional, for instance, to remove your shoes before entering the homes of Malays, Indians and Chinese. Pointing your foot

Above: multi-culturalism is a unique aspect of the city **Top right:** soccer-mad Malaysian youths **Right:** Masjid Jamek is an important place of worship for Muslims

at anybody is considered an insult by all three races. Among Malays, it is considered impolite to converse in a loud and raucous manner, but the Indians and Chinese are not too sensitive about this. The list goes on.

The religious practices of Muslims are central to their lives. Most pray five times a day and many offices have prayer rooms (*surau*). Eating with one's left hand is also considered inappropriate by both Muslims and Hindus. Probably one of the most delightful aspects of KL's multiculturalism is the 'open house'. This is where people from different races visit each other during the respective cultural celebrations. Celebrants open their houses to visitors all day long during the festive period, and there is always food on hand regardless of whether or not it is mealtime. These periods are also when the city folk discard their usual Western-style office wear for more traditional ethnic or ethnic-inspired garb. There are a number of books on handling culture shock in Kuala Lumpur *(see Practical Information, page 91)*. When in doubt, ask politely. Most KL-ites (as the people call themselves) are friendly and will not hesitate to help out visitors to their city.

A Safe City, but …

Relative to other Southeast Asian capitals such as Jakarta and Bangkok, Kuala Lumpur is a safe city for visitors. The Internal Security Act, brainchild of the British colonialists to fight the Communist threat in the 1960s, allows detention without trial of anyone who threatens national security. This law, still in force today, muzzles the press and restricts access to official in-

formation. Nonetheless, it is the memory and fear of a repeat of post-election racial riots that took lives and rocked the city on 13 May 1969 that keep Malaysians supine. The result was the New Economic Policy, aimed at closing the economic disparity between the urban Chinese and the growing Malay middle class. This goal has been achieved to some extent through intensive industrialisation and private-public sector alliances, spearheaded by former Prime Minister Mahathir Mohamad during his 1981–2003 term in office.

A decade of nearly 10 per cent annual economic growth rates in the 1990s is seeing a Kuala Lumpur and Malaysia that is educated, affluent and global in outlook, yet with peculiar quirks and attitudes that can only be described as nothing else but Malaysian. While the country struggles to maintain its moderate Islamic image on the world stage in the face of the current waves of Muslim terrorism, its capital is also working at becoming a 'world-class city', in terms of living, working and business environments. This goal is embodied in the KL Structure Plan 2020, which re-examines policies about living, income, population, land use, development, trading and tourism.

For tourists, snatch theft and pick-pockets are probably what they should be most careful about. As in all cities, be careful in crowded areas and when taking public transport; women should be careful not to walk around alone after midnight, and to steer clear of alleys and poorly-lit places.

Orientation

Right in the old heart of Kuala Lumpur is the colonial core around the Padang, where the Brits used to hang out; the new heart east of that is the Kuala Lumpur City Centre (KLCC), home to the Petronas Twin Tower spires. Next to the old heart is Chinatown, and north of this is Chow Kit. Head west and you hit the Malay enclave of Kampung Bahru. South of the KLCC is the shopping and commercial centre of Bukit Bintang, which sits in the constantly developing area known as the Golden Triangle.

Above: central Kuala Lumpur and Chinatown

HISTORY HIGHLIGHTS

1403 Malacca Sultanate begins when Parameswara flees from Sumatra to Malacca. Advent of Islam.

1857 Kuala Lumpur is founded by tin miners and becomes a staging point for the trading of tin. Chinese labour is imported.

1867 Selangor is torn by civil war over the imposition of export duties on tin ore. The war spreads to KL and in 1872, the city is razed to the ground.

1868–1885 Yap Ah Loy becomes 'Kapitan China' of Kuala Lumpur, develops the town and contributes significantly to the city's growth

1882 Frank Swettenham is appointed Resident of Selangor, and continues its development. The KL-Klang railway line is built. KL's Malay and Indian population increases.

1890s Indian Moorish architecture style introduced to Kuala Lumpur.

1895 Formation of the Federated Malay States.

1896 Kuala Lumpur is declared the capital of the Federated Malay States by the British.

1941–45 Japanese occupy the Malay Peninsula.

1946 Rise of Malay nationalism. United Malays National Organisation (UMNO) is formed on 1 March.

1948 Federation of Malaya is created. State of Emergency declared because of communist insurgency.

1951 The Malayan Chinese Association (MCA) forms a partnership with UMNO.

1953 The Malayan Indian Congress (MIC) joins the UMNO-MCA partnership, forming the Barisan Nasional (Alliance), which plays a major role in the country's independence struggle.

1955 In Malaya's first national election, the Alliance wins 80 percent of the votes cast.

1957 On 31 August, Malaya becomes an independent nation, with Tunku Abdul Rahman as its first Prime Minister. Kuala Lumpur is made the capital of Malaya.

1961 Year-long state of Emergency is declared over the communist threat.

1963 On 16 September, Singapore, Sabah and Sarawak join Malaysia and KL becomes the national capital.

1965 Singapore withdraws from Malaysia to become a republic.

1970 Tun Abdul Razak is Malaysia's second Prime Minister. New Economic Policy for economic restructuring is introduced.

1972 Kuala Lumpur is accorded city status.

1974 KL is annexed from Selangor to become the Federal Territory.

1975 Tun Hussein Onn takes over as Prime Minister.

1981 Datuk Seri Dr Mahathir Mohamad is elected Prime Minister.

1986 The Proton Saga, the first locally manufactured automobile, rolls off the assembly line.

1991 The more liberal New Development Policy (Vision 2020) takes effect. It aims to make Malaysia a developed country by 2020.

1996 Malaysia launches its first satellite, the Measat I.

1997 Completion of the 450-m-tall (1,480-ft) Petronas Twin Towers, the world's tallest twin buildings to date.

1998 KL hosts the XVI Commonwealth Games. The economy takes a stumble and currency controls are imposed.

1999 Federal government's offices move to the new administrative centre in Putrajaya. Economy rebounds.

2001 Kuala Lumpur Draft Structure Plan 2000–2020 prepared.

2003 Datuk Seri Abdullah Ahmad Badawi is nominated Malaysia's fifth Prime Minister.

2004 KL Structure Plan 2020, which focusses on urban growth and development, is gazetted.

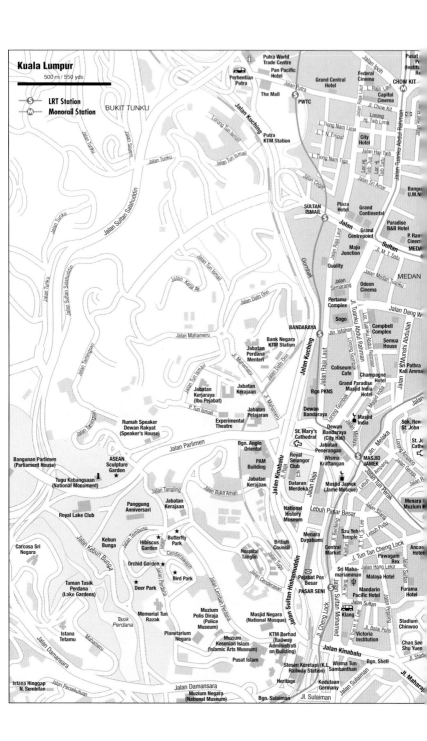

Kuala Lumpur

500 m / 550 yds

Ⓢ LRT Station
Ⓜ Monorail Station

BUKIT TUNKU

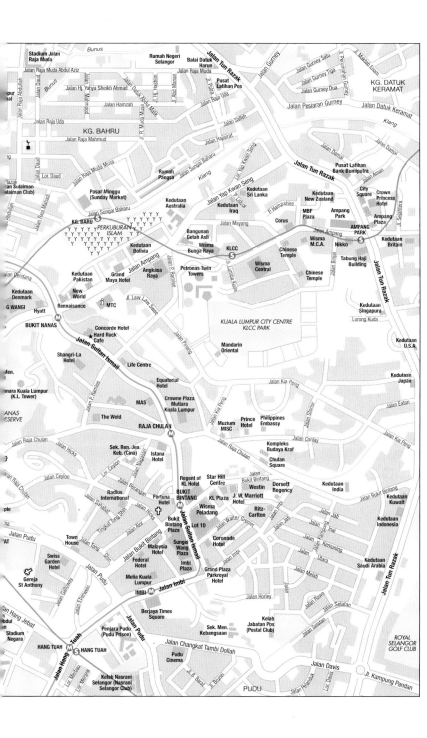

City
Itineraries

T
he unrelenting pace of construction is what still gives Kuala Lumpur (KL) the feel of a booming city despite being over 150 years old. Much of the new development centres on flyovers and the public rail transport system. Recent massive redevelopment projects include the Kuala Lumpur City Centre (KLCC) in the heart of the prestigious Golden Triangle area, the financial and commercial district: the Petronas Twin Towers are only the first of a host of other structures planned in that area.

The first three days in KL should be allocated to orienting yourself to this cosmopolitan city. This is reflected in the first three full-day itineraries in this guide. The first allows you to appreciate Kuala Lumpur's historic origins; the second, its present role as a thriving marketplace; and the third, to reflect upon its quieter, greener areas.

Itineraries 4–11 are half- or full-day options that are a guide to KL's different faces and cater to various interests. KL wears a different face during the day from the night, and while the itineraries include a suggestion of best times to visit, it is sometimes worthwhile going back to the same place in the evening. The city assumes a different aura again during festivities, particularly at its various ethnic hubs to which the festivals are pertinent, for instance, Kampung Bahru during the Muslim Hari Raya Puasa, and Chinatown during Chinese New Year.

While the itineraries highlight most of the main attractions, various nooks and crannies tucked away in between looming skyscrapers can reveal interesting insights into the city. It is generally safe to give in to your exploratory instincts during the day, although the usual commonsense safety rules apply.

For visitors with more time, six excursions *(pages 53–63)* to places outside of the city proper take you to cool highland resorts and rustic islands.

Hot-footing It

Most of KL's attractions are accessible by foot, although pedestrian walkways were obviously not a top priority on the town builders' agendas. Heavy traffic and pollution do not help. Nonetheless, walking is the quickest way to get around during gridlock rush hours, and especially when it rains. Therefore, if possible, avoid road transport between 7–9am and 4–7pm on weekdays, and 1–2pm on Saturdays. For those not used to the humidity, start the half-day itineraries early and aim to finish up by noon.

To travel between attractions, hop into a taxi, or the air-conditioned Light Rail Transport System (LRT), Monorail or KTM Komuter electric trains. A network of trains and buses also bring you to attractions outside of the city centre. Alternatively, book a taxi for the day. Many of the attractions covered in this guide are also part of guided bus tours from KL.

Left: Sultan Abdul Samad building
Right: a schoolgirl with national flag

1. GETTING ACQUAINTED *(see map below)*

A full day, starting with breakfast at Medan Pasar Lama; explore the historic hub with its Moorish-inspired buildings, then stroll to the Kuala Lumpur Railway Station. End the day with dinner at the Central Market.

Take the LRT to Pasar Seni, cross the road towards the Central Market and walk past it till you reach a square. This is Medan Pasar Lama, the starting point.

This tour is designed to give you a feel of the city, from its origins as a colonial outpost to the thriving metropolis it is today. Start with a breakfast of steamed – not toasted – bread and *kaya* (a delicious jam of coconut and eggs)

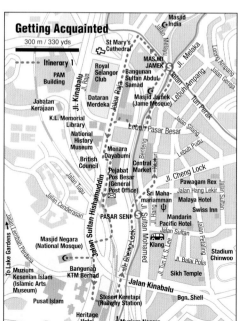

at the **Sin Seng Nam Restaurant** (closed on Sunday) at **Medan Pasar Lama**. The square is one of the oldest parts of the city, its Georgio-Romanesque facades resplendent, if somewhat incongruous with its surroundings, in the morning sun. This is where the city's first brick buildings were erected in the late 19th century under British Resident Frank Swettenham.

After breakfast, walk down the square towards the Hong Kong Bank Building (opposite the Bank of Tokyo and Mitsubishi) and turn left. You are now at **Benteng**, and can clearly see the confluence

Above: Dataran Merdeka is the city's historic centre

of two rivers – the Gombak and Klang – that give the city its name. Head along Benteng where there is a mini bazaar, till you reach Jalan Tun Perak, then turn left. To the left of the Benteng LRT Station you will find the entrance to **Masjid Jamek** (Jamek Mosque), a sprawl of colonnades and spires around a peaceful square. This beautiful building is the city's oldest mosque.

Moorish Influence

Further down, on the same side of the street, you will come to the city's most regal neighbourhood, despite the thrust of the LRT line. Done in Moorish majesty, these blocks of colonial buildings around the **Padang** (Town Green) comprise the historical heart of Kuala Lumpur city. This is where the British administrators of the Federated Malay States built their headquarters in the 1890s. For some reason, the colonial architects of the Public Works Department deemed the Moghul style of architecture appropriate for the government buildings of the Malay Peninsula. The distinct style is completely imported from another British outpost, India. The building facing Jalan Tun Perak houses the **Sessions and Magistrates Courts**.

Turn left at the junction with Jalan Raja. On the left is the former colonial administrative centre, the **Bangunan Sultan Abdul Samad**, now the Supreme Court, and one of the most photographed of the city's landmarks. Come back again at night to see this magnificent building lit up; it is a pretty sight indeed. The road in front of this building, Jalan Raja, is off limits to traffic on Saturday nights when youngsters, lovers, and families hang out here or stroll along the road, enjoying the night breeze and bright lights.

The Padang is also the focus of the annual countdown to Hari Merdeka (Independence Day); and at the stroke of midnight, the big clock at Bangunan Sultan Abdul Samad strikes to herald 31 August. On 31 December every year, large crowds also gather here to count down to the New Year.

Directly opposite the Bangunan Sultan Abdul Samad across the Padang is a cluster of Tudor-style buildings. This is another colonial relic, the members-only **Royal Selangor Club** (circa 1884), which prides itself on an ambience that dates back to the days when Somerset Maugham was a regular visitor. The Padang is used for occasional cricket games, although cricket never really caught on in this country, unlike many other British colonies.

The massive plaza to the left of the Padang is the **Dataran Merdeka** (Independence Square), anchored by one of the world's tallest flagpoles and a giant video screen. It was here at midnight on 31 August 1957 that England's Union Jack was lowered for the last time (on a humbler and shorter flagpole) and Malaysia became an independent state. Around the Padang are several other colonial buildings which have been restored and turned into museums, notably the **Muzium Sejarah Nasional** (National History

Right: fountain detail at Dataran Merdeka

Museum; open daily 9am–6pm) and the **Kuala Lumpur Memorial Library**.

There are two options from here. Across the busy Jalan Kinabalu on Jalan Tangsi is another colonial gem dating back to 1907. The **PAM Building** hosts the Persaturan Arkitek Malaysia (Architect's Association of Malaysia) and the Galeri Tangsi Art Gallery. You might want to cool off with a beer and fill your tummy with a set lunch at the restaurant and pub here, **Charlie's Place** (tel: 03-2693 3975; open 12pm–12am; closed Sun). It also has a cosy garden setting which is quite pleasant in the evenings. Back at the Padang facing the Bangunan Sultan Abdul Samad, a quiet little church sits on the far left, **St Mary's Cathedral**, which was built in the Gothic tradition in 1894 and one of the oldest Anglican churches in the region. Services are still held here.

Islamic Influences

Head back to Jalan Raja, and veer left. You will come to the gleaming white **Menara Dayabumi** (Dayabumi Complex), with its fine filigree-like Islamic design. It is at its most impressive at night when it is floodlit. Go past the **General Post Office** or **POS Malaysia** (tel: 03-2274 1122; open Mon–Sat 8.30am–4pm, closed Sun and first Sat of each month), and take the pedestrian subway to the other side of Jalan Sultan Hishamuddin.

Ahead is the **Masjid Negara** (National Mosque; open Sat–Thurs 9am–6pm, Fri 3–6pm) with its 73-m (240-ft) tall minaret and geometric lattice-work. Resplendent in white marble offset by pools of gurgling water, the National Mosque accommodates up to 10,000 people at a time. If you wish to enter the mosque, remove your shoes and use the robe provided if you are wearing shorts. Tour the interior to see the ornamental pools, fountains, a gallery, the library and the Grand Prayer Hall. Tourists, however, are forbidden from entering the Prayer Hall.

Down the road from the mosque on the right is the last of the Moghul-style buildings to be constructed, the **Bangunan KTM Berhad** (Railway Administration Building), an architectural stunner. Another Moorish architecture extravagance, the **Stesen Keretapi Kuala Lumpur** (Kuala Lumpur Railway Station) stands opposite, and can be accessed by an underground pass

beneath the busy road. The building is part of the city's proud efforts at architectural preservation. First completed in 1885, it was rebuilt at the turn of the century. It was subsequently extensively renovated in the 1980s. However, the bustle of moving bodies and luggage has vanished since the interstate rail services were moved to the glitzy new Kuala Lumpur transport hub at KL Sentral Station.

Walk through the railway station to get to Jalan Cheng Lock. From Platform 1, head right until you reach a subway and head for the exit on Platform 4. Occasionally, late at night, the famous and very expensive cream-and-green Eastern and Oriental Express *(see Practical Information, page 79)* train passes through on its way from Singapore in the south on its way to Butterworth, Bangkok and Chiang Mai up north (or vice versa). On a much more mundane level, the KTM Komuter trains head out from the centre platform to Port Klang, Seremban and Rawang.

Hand-made Goodies

You will now be facing **Jalan Cheng Lock**. Turn left and walk some 500m (546yds) to the landmark **Central Market** (Pasar Seni). Once the city's largest wet-produce market, this was converted in the late 1980s into a cultural-cum-shopping mall. Its art deco features and its high ceilings were recently renovated and repainted. This is a great place to shop for souvenirs. A good variety of goods are sold here, including handicrafts, souvenirs, antiques and art, all at fairly reasonable prices. Be sure to bargain for your purchases though. Artists are also on hand at the mall to draw caricatures or portraits on the spot. Pick up a brochure here or at the tourist office, and you may be lucky enough to catch a music, dance or shadow puppet performance for free.

Just outside, a pedestrian mall fronts quaint old shops selling dried fish, rice wine and Taoist icons. At the back is another row of pre-war buildings turned souvenir shops and restaurants. Central Market is a popular hangout for Malay youth, particularly boys and young men. It is not rare to see guitarists among them, testament to the fact that this was the birthplace of the local underground music scene, comprising mainly rock bands whose hole-in-the-knee and faded jeans-clad members are known locally as *Mat Rock*.

For dinner, head for **Restaurant Ginger** (tel: 03-2273 7371) upstairs at the Central Market for specialities like spicy Malay *rendang* beef curry and Thai green chicken curry served with rice. You can also cool down with a beer in its charming wooden interior.

eft: a lasting British legacy is the KL Railway Station **Top and Right:** traditional 'Ialaysian *wau bulan* (moon kite) and a Chinese painter at Central Market

2. CHINATOWN *(see map, p27)*

A full-day tour starting at a money museum; walk down atmospheric Petaling Street; have a Chinese vegetarian lunch; visit Hindu and Chinese temples; and end the evening with dinner at a Nyonya restaurant.

Starting point is the Muzium Numismatik in the Menara Maybank tower. Take the LRT to the Plaza Rakyat Station, walk past the Puduraya Bus and Taxi Station, and cross the road to Menara Maybank, diagonally opposite.

Chinatown in Kuala Lumpur is similar to Chinatowns everywhere in the world (except perhaps China) – a colourful collage of earthy people, colourful temples and shops, and noisy restaurants.

Start the day by visiting a money museum, the **Muzium Numismatik** or Numismatic Museum (open daily 10am–6pm), located in the rear lobby of **Menara Maybank** (Malayan Banking Building) on Jalan Tun Perak. The museum has a good collection of old coins and notes dating back to early Malaya.

After you're done, walk towards the chaotic **Puduraya Bus and Taxi Station**. This is where interstate buses and taxis leave for destinations throughout the peninsula, Singapore and Thailand. There are small hotels in the building itself and close by, convenient for late night arrivals or early morning departures. Before you reach Puduraya, turn right into **Jalan Cheng Lock** (on your right is the **Mydin** wholesale emporium). Cross Jalan Cheng Lock at the traffic lights to get to **Jalan Sultan**. Ahead sprawls the Chinatown district.

Chinatown is concentrated in Jalan Petaling, Jalan Tun H S Lee and Jalan Hang Lekir. It is usually referred to as Petaling Street, the main thoroughfare of which is cordoned off for a popular night market from 6pm to

Top: deity at Persatuan Kwong Siew Chinese Temple *(see page 28)*
Above: mooncakes are sold only during the Lantern Festival in September

city itineraries

midnight. Typical of Chinatowns, there are medicine shops with jars of dried roots and herbs, and other products of less salubrious origins. There are sidewalk palm readers and fortune tellers perched on stools and whose 'tools' are laid out in open briefcases. There are tea houses and art shops, coffin makers and hidden temples, pet shops and flower vendors. A large number of stores sell cheap clothing, and backpacker accommodation is plentiful here; Chinatown is definitely a focus for tourists.

Fascinating Facets

Interestingly, the character of Chinatown changes through the day. In the morning, people throng *dim sum* restaurants for breakfast and the wet market is active with housewives picking at the fresh produce. In the afternoon, there is a lull, but from 5pm, **Jalan Petaling** is closed to traffic and makeshift stalls take over the road with rapid efficiency. As darkness falls, and particularly on weekends, Chinatown's atmosphere is almost electric. City folk and tourists alike are drawn to bargains in the *pasar malam* (night market) or to sample the excellent food by the roadside or on the 'five-foot-way'(the local term for a shaded footpath). And well into the wee hours of the morning, long after most stall-owners have packed up, late-nighters, some bleary-eyed from night-clubbing, have their suppers under the bright fluorescent lights of a few late-night stalls. For this reason, you may want to start this tour in the afternoon instead, so that you can experience nightfall here.

From Jalan Sultan, head past the Rex Cinema and turn right into **Jalan Hang Lekir**, lined with shops selling dried pork floss and other Chinese delicacies. Stop at one of the many Chinese restaurants at the Jalan Petaling intersection and have a typical Chinese snack. There are many noodle dishes to try out, including soupy rice noodles or the soya sauce base *kon loh* style. You could also have a go at *pau*, Chinese dumplings with meat or bean paste fillings, or *bak-kut teh*, which is a fragrant stew of pork ribs and herbs. Food in Chinatown is usually not halal and therefore taboo for Muslims.

Just down the street, Jalan Hang Lekir meets Jalan Petaling. The latter is not just chaotic; it is pure anarchy. Here, sidewalk vendors and pedestrians compete with cars negotiating the narrow road. Shopping here is an exciting, even heady experience but some people find it exhausting. This is also delightful fodder for the camera-happy, but photographers would do

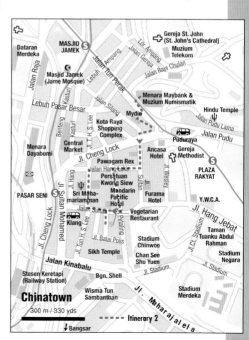

well to ask permission before taking photos as many people object.

There are a couple of things you should know about shopping in Chinatown. First, to get the best price, bargain enthusiastically. Second, despite whatever you are told, it is not the place for designer labels. You may see vendors hawking Gucci handbags and Cartier watches which look uncannily like the real thing, but they are clever rip-offs, sometimes right down to the warranty cards.

To get to your lunch spot, walk down Jalan Petaling towards Jalan Sultan. Turn right at Jalan Sultan and after about 50m (165ft), turn left into a small alley called **Jalan Panggung**, just before the Ocean Supermarket. Walk down another 50m (165ft) and you will reach **Wan Fo Yuan Vegetarian Restaurant** where you can try a reasonably-priced Chinese vegetarian meal. Chinese vegetarian cooking is an art form in its own right. The food is made to resemble meat or fish (and sometimes even tastes like the real McCoy) but is made entirely from soya bean gluten.

Chinatown's Hindu Temple

After lunch, turn right and head back towards Jalan Sultan, where you turn left and walk towards the junction with **Jalan Tun H S Lee**. Turn right at this junction and you will see the **Sri Mahamariamman Hindu Temple** (open daily 8am–6pm) on the left side of the road. The temple is an arresting sight, all the more for its incongruent setting in this Chinese enclave. Built in 1873, the temple occupies an important place in Hindu religious life, as it is from here that the annual Thaipusam pilgrimage to Batu Caves *(see Itinerary 9)* begins. Remove your footwear first if you decide to enter the temple. Outside, vendors sell fragrant jasmine flowers strung into garlands.

Further down on the right side of the road is the **Persatuan Kwong Siew Chinese Temple** (open daily 7am–5pm), built by the Kwong Siew Association in 1888. Watch devotees make incense offerings, but be especially mindful of when and who you photograph. There is usually a donation box and a nominal donation is always appreciated.

After this, continue your shopping spree, and end the evening at **Jalan Balai Polis**, where beautifully preserved shophouses have become trendy among young Chinese. Dine on Nyonya food in a former laundry association, now the **Old China Café and Antique Shop**. Go through swinging doors into a decidedly old world atmosphere, where black-and-white photos deck the walls and food is served on heavy marble-topped tables.

Above: a Chinese favourite – grilled dried pork slices
Right: gateway to Sri Mahamariamman Hindu Temple

3. LAKE GARDENS AND THE MUSEUMS *(see map, p30)*

Another full-day: begin with a Malay breakfast; morning stroll around the lush Lake Gardens; a spicy Indian lunch eaten off banana leaves; spend the humid afternoon in museums; and party at night in Bangsar.

Starting point is a back entrance to the Lake Gardens on Jalan Cender-awasih, accessible from the National Mosque. The closest KTM Komuter train or LRT stop is the KL Sentral Station; taxis are plentiful here.

Alfred Venning, the former British State Treasurer, was more interested in the idea of creating a paradisiacal botanical garden amid lakes in the heart of Kuala Lumpur than with making money. Now, over 120 years later, the name Venning scarcely means anything to most KL-ites, but his legacy strikes deep in the heart of the city. The **Lake Gardens** (Taman Tasik Perdana; open Mon–Sat 9am–6pm, Sun and public holidays 8am–6pm), with its 104ha (257 acres) of close-cropped lawns, undulating hills and carefully cultivated gardens, is a sanctuary from the maddening mayhem of the city. The leafy Lake Gardens is also a valuable green lung, helping to cleanse the city of its polluted air.

Start the day early, with a typical local breakfast on the fringes of the Lake Gardens. Tell the taxi driver to take you to Jalan Cenderawasih, on the left and off Jalan Sultan Hishamuddin after the National Mosque. Get off in front of Tanglin Hospital. Directly opposite is a small hawker centre where you can dine on *nasi lemak*, a Malaysian meal of fragrant rice cooked in coconut milk with side dishes like *ikan bilis sambal* (anchovies cooked with chillies), *rendang* (beef cooked with spices and coconut milk), peanuts and cucumber. The stall is closed on Sunday.

The Lake Gardens are popular with health nuts at dawn and dusk, and you get the range from Nike-clad joggers to tai-chi exponents. On Sunday mornings, a free communal aerobics session to blasting music is held in the Panggung Aniversari ampitheatre. Weekends see mums, dads and kids throng the area, maids in tow and picnic baskets in hand; this is a good opportunity to watch Malaysian families at play.

bove: the Butterfly Park is home to some 6,000 winged creatures

Flora and Fauna

Apart from the gardens, there are other attractions in the area, including the Deer Park with several local species; Bird Park, one of the region's largest aviaries; Butterfly Park, a sanctuary for some 6,000 winged creatures of over 120 species; Orchid Garden and Hibiscus Garden, with hundreds of luxuriant blooms.

You won't have time to visit all the parks in a few hours so take this suggested route. Start early in the morning when it is fresh. For those who eschew traipsing around in the hot, humid conditions, there is a park shuttle bus (operates daily 9am–7pm with a break at lunchtime) that will take you to the main attractions. After breakfast, walk 200m (660ft) up the road to the **Butterfly Park** (tel: 03-2693 4799; open daily 9am–6pm). This pretty landscaped garden is a delight to stroll through. There is also a building housing Malaysia's weird and wonderful collection of tropical rainforest insects, reptiles and amphibians – masters of adaptation and camouflage.

Continue to the **Hibiscus Garden** (open daily 9am–6pm), a 10-minute walk up Jalan Cenderawasih, where it meets Jalan Tembusu. Malaysian forests harbour several species of this lovely bloom. However, for some reason, the species that was chosen as Malaysia's national flower (*bunga raya*) and appears on Malaysian coins, is actually not native to the country, having originated from either China or India.

Then follow the signs to the **Bird Park** (tel: 03-2272 1010; open daily 9am–7.30pm). This 8-ha (20-acre) covered aviary is home to 3,000 birds of over 200 species. Most are free-flying except for raptors and certain

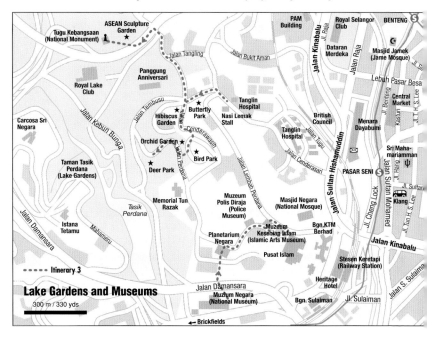

species which are housed in display and confined areas. Of note is the hornbill section, where you get close-up views of these large black and white creatures with prominent beaks and magnificent tails. Malaysia has 10 species of hornbills, some of which figure in the rites and beliefs of certain indigenous people.

Opposite the Bird Park is the **Orchid Garden** (open daily 9am–6pm), which celebrates this largest of flowering plant families. Malaysia has among the most diverse orchid species in the world (around 2,000). Some of these are grown here in this garden, which has 800-odd species, a mixture of both cultivated and wild orchids, and many specimens are on sale.

When you are done with the Orchid Garden, turn right and walk on until you reach the T-junction, then take a right again to get to the Deer Park. On your left, the **Tun Razak's Memorial** is a tribute to Malaysia's second Prime Minister. The **Deer Park** (open daily 9am–6pm) will appeal especially to children. The highlight is the mousedeer, the smallest deer in the world, which is the size of a cat, and extremely shy, so scour the brush carefully to spot it.

Backtrack to Jalan Cenderawasih and walk to Jalan Parlimen, which ends on the left at the Parliament House (not open to the public). The **Tugu Kebangsaan** (National Monument) is across Jalan Parlimen and commemorates those who died during the Communist insurgency of the 1950s. The adjacent ASEAN **Sculpture Garden** features sculptures from the region (ASEAN is a regional economic and political association).

Lunch Options

As it will be lunchtime, you have a choice: a genteel colonial English atmosphere or an earthy South Indian experience. For the former, walk to the gracious **Carcosa Seri Negara** hotel (tel: 03-2282 1888) on Persiaran Mahameru. From the Tugu Kebangsaan, cross the road back to the Lake Gardens but turn right and follow the main road till you come to a turning to the left. Follow this road uphill and you will come to some charming whitewashed mansions on your right.

If it's a Sunday, the Carcosa's curry tiffins at **Gulai House** are worth trying out. Enjoy French cuisine at its **Mahsuri Dining Room** or outside in rattan chairs on the garden-facing verandahs. The mock-Tudor Carcosa, which was built in 1896, was once the residence of top British officials, and is now a luxury hotel. If you don't feel like lunching here (there is a dress code), consider returning at some point of your stay for English tea with scones and cucumber sandwiches at **The Drawing Room**, or a candle-lit gourmet dinner.

For the simpler no-frills lunch alternative, take a taxi to **Brickfields**, just 2km (1¼ miles) or a 10-minute ride away. Try a typical South Indian lunch, eaten off a banana leaf, at **Sri Devi Restaurant** at 9 Jalan Travers (tel: 03-2260 1553). Ask for steamed plain rice, *beryani* (fragrant basmati rice), or *thosai* (rice flour-based pancakes). There is a variety of side dishes to accompany the meal. Lentil gravy and vegetables

Top left: Bird Park's flamingos
Right: the National Monument

come with the rice or *thosai,* and the spicy, dry mutton curry is highly recommended. In true South Indian style, the meal is eaten with the fingers of the right hand only, but ask for cutlery if you wish. Wash the meal down with a glass of cold *lassi*, a yoghurt-based drink. To end the meal, indulge in sweets like *jelebi, mysore pak* or *ladu*, but dieters be warned that these are loaded with sugar and milk.

A Motley of Museums

From Brickfields, take a taxi to the **Muzium Negara** (National Museum; open daily 9am–6pm) – or walk from the Carcosa Seri Negara if you lunched there – and spend a couple of hours soaking up Malaysian history, local culture, and arts and craft. Its social and cultural sections include the Nyonyas and Babas (also known as Peranakan), the unique fusion of Chinese and Malay races. The museum features some offbeat exhibits – such as cats and treasures from dug-up graves, and the skull of an elephant which is said to have derailed a train in Malaysia.

The museum is small enough not to require a guided tour. The building itself is of interest, influenced by the old Malay *kampung* (village) house, and topped by the 'buffalo-horned' Minangkabau-style roof. Two massive Italian murals depict the highlights of Malaysian history.

A pedestrian bridge behind the museum leads to the **Planetarium Negara** (National Planetarium; open Tue–Sun 9.30am–4.15pm). The planetarium has a 36-cm (14-inch) telescope and a theatre, and also houses the Arianne IV space engine which launched Malaysia's first satellite, the Measat I. Its well-designed garden is scattered with replicas of ancient observatories.

If you are keen on more museums or it happens to be a rainy day, turn right into Jalan Perdana to get to the **Muzium Polis Diraja Malaysia** (Royal Malaysian Police Museum; open Tue–Sun 10am–6pm). In the grounds, kids will enjoy exploring armoured tanks and the Police Force's first aircraft – a single-engined Cessna. The most popular displays in the museum's three galleries are in the Weapons section, featuring guns confiscated from post-World War II China-aligned Communist guerillas, and wicked-looking Secret Society weapons.

Down the road is a must-see: the **Muzium Kesenian Islam Malaysia** (Islamic Arts Museum Malaysia; tel: 03-2274 2020; www.iamm.org.my; open Tue–Sun 10am–6pm). From the Police Museum, walk down Jalan Perdana and turn left into Jalan Lembah Perdana to get to the main entrance. This is a dignified and spacious privately-owned repository of artefacts and art objects from the Islamic world, with temporary exhibitions in the lower floors and permanent collections in the two upper floors.

Of note are the intricate architectural models of famous monuments and structures of the Islamic era, such as the Indian Taj Mahal and famous mosques of the holy city of Medinah. Careful reconstruction

Left: Islamic Arts Museum

also went into the Ottoman Room, which harks back to what is generally considered as the Renaissance of Islamic Arts (1453–1923). Other displays range from manuscripts to ceramics, and metalwork to arms.

There are also facilities for children, and an impressive shop selling textiles, artwork, books, crystal and replicas of artifacts from all over the Islamic world. Have a coffee and snack at the café, or dine at its Middle Eastern restaurant (tel: 03-2273 1794; 12pm–10pm).

Bangsar Nightlife

For dinner, take a taxi to **Bangsar** and you won't be short on choice of food from any part of the world. It's all here – from Spanish *tapas* to Italian gourmet meals, from Northern Indian breads to pizza, and from hair-curling spicy Thai curries to English pub grub.

After your meal, take a walk around Bangsar, the city's definitive area for KL's trendy. Lined with wall-to-wall pubs, coffeehouses and beautiful people, this is also a popular hangout for expatriates. Fridays and Saturdays are packed, and although weekenders indulge mainly in drinking and people-watching, tiny dance clubs blasting techno and house music are the latest fixtures to take hold. Then again, tomorrow might find them gone, such are the dictates of the fickle-minded Bangsarian. Among the survivors of whim are the regularly patronised pubs – Canteena's, Ronnie Q's and the Irish Finnegan's – as well as the trend-setting Modesto's, Alexis Bistro and La Bodega Tapas Y Vinos.

Located at Jalan Ara, **Bangsar Village** features a mall with trendy cafés, specialist shops and restaurants, and it is popular among locals. Just as heavily frequented is **Bangsar Shopping Centre**, which is situated at the end of Jalan Maaraf.

At the evening's end, sober up with a hot local 'pulled' tea (*teh tarik*) and spicy mutton soup. Head for the alley of open-air Indian and Malay stalls, called the Bangsar stalls, which are crowded from the time they set up shop at dinnertime till the early hours of the morning.

Trendy goes underground briefly on Sunday evenings when the itinerant stalls of the *pasar malam* (night market) take over the streets. Locals from the surrounding neighbourhoods emerge to shop for everything from vegetables to pirated CDs and cheap plastic toys. However, because this is Bangsar, designer labels are evident, the makeup immaculate, and chic black becomes prominent as twilight deepens into night.

city itineraries

bove: Bangsar's Telawi Street Bistro

4. CHOW KIT *(see map below)*

Shop at The Mall and have dinner at Medan Hang Tuah; walk down Chow Kit; and browse at an open-air bazaar. This is a three-hour tour.

Start at The Mall, close to the Putra World Trade Centre. To get there, take the KTM Komuter to the Putra Station, walk out and turn left and follow the road downhill. The Mall is on your right. Early evening is a good time to do this route.

Mention **Chow Kit** to any KL-ite and watch the sly grins spreading over their faces. There is a good reason for it, Chow Kit was once the most notorious neighbourhood in the city. Today, urban renewal has sanitised much of what was once KL's sleaze centre. But old impressions die hard. Besides, such things are not easily suppressed. In the backlanes and dark alleys of a Chow Kit evening, transvestites still ply their trade and call girls stare from behind masks of cheap make-up.

To experience the two contrasting faces of Chow Kit, begin your walk at the chic shopping plaza, **The Mall**, at the end of **Jalan Putra**. Opposite The Mall is the sprawling **Putra World Trade Centre** (PWTC) where consumer and trade exhibitions are held. Inside this complex are the headquarters of UMNO, the ruling political party, a concert venue, and the Tourism Malaysia headquarters. Tourist information is available at its office on the ground floor.

On the other side of Jalan Putra from the PWTC is **Perhentian Putra**, the bus station for express coaches to and from the east coast of the peninsula. Adjacent to the PWTC is the **Pan Pacific Hotel**, where you can sample local hawker fare in its air-conditioned brasserie, **Selera Restaurant** (tel: 03-4049 4351), while observing the bustle along Jalan Putra.

The Mall houses a host of shops, including the Parkson Grand department store, which has a decent range of clothing. Taking up almost half of

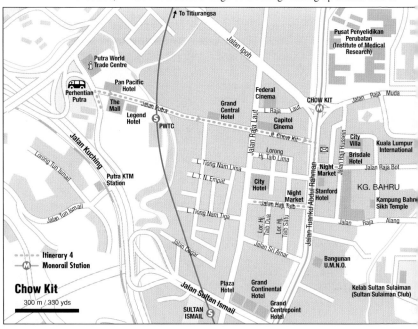

the fourth floor is a food court called **Medan Hang Tuah**. Modelled on the Kuala Lumpur of the 1930s, doorways, street lights and building facades have been painstakingly recreated. The food court offers an immense variety of Malay and Chinese food. Have an early dinner here.

Adjoining The Mall is the **Legend Hotel**, which has an excellent if expensive fine dining Chinese restaurant, **The Museum** (tel: 03-4042 9888), and the **Monkey Bar**, where you occasionally get good bands. Then head down Jalan Putra towards **Jalan Chow Kit**, about a 15-minute walk or a short taxi ride away. Continue past the crossroads to **Jalan Tuanku Abdul Rahman**. The Chow Kit Bus Stand here is where you can get buses to the trendy and upmarket suburb of Bangsar *(see page 33)* for a completely different cosmopolitan experience. Buses from here also go to Jalan Genting Kelang, and to the National Zoo and Aquarium. From here onwards, you will find no greater contrast to your earlier experience at the Mall. Remember to be careful with your personal belongings.

Start on the side of the road you are now on and walk in the direction of the traffic. All the stores lining the street have cheap goods. When the pavement becomes noticeably crowded with vendors, weave your way through and turn left into **Jalan Raja Bot**. This lane is lined with Malay food vendors and stalls selling cheap goods. Where it ends at Brisdale Hotel, turn back and retrace your steps to Jalan Tuanku Abdul Rahman. Continue walking until you reach a pedestrian crossing. Further down this road is the start of the Kampung Bahru itinerary *(see page 43)*. Cross to the other side of the road and head for **Jalan Haji Taib**, the Malay version of the Chinatown night market.

The range of goods here is not as extensive as in Chinatown. Bargain items are mainly RM5 jeans, a mixture of imported goods from Thailand, reject clothing from factories, or second-hand denims from the US. You can also get leather goods and pirated VCDs as well as T-shirts. However, as with any night market, do not be deceived by fake designer labels and brands. If prices seem inflated, bargain.

Above: a cosmetics shop at The Mall
Right: an ethnic crafts shop

5. JALAN TUANKU ABDUL RAHMAN *(see map below)*

Start this half-day tour with lunch at the Coliseum Café; wander down Jalan Tuanku Abdul Rahman and explore the Masjid India area; visit Little India and enjoy a North Indian dinner.

Starting point is the Coliseum Café and Hotel. Take the LRT to the Bandaraya LRT Station or the KTM Komuter to the Bank Negara Station. Walk towards the Sogo departmental store, go past it, and turn left when you reach Jalan Tuanku Abdul Rahman. Continue until you reach the Coliseum. This is recommended as an afternoon tour.

Built in 1928, the **Coliseum Café and Hotel** (tel: 03-2692 6270) located next to the Coliseum Cinema on Jalan Tuanku Abdul Rahman has definitely seen better days. Its original decor, and mismatched furniture and fittings disguise a once popular drinking hole for prosperous colonial planters, tin miners and traders. It still serves good, hearty meals served by old and sullen-faced Hainanese Chinese waiters, traditionally chefs for the colonials, and makes for an interesting (and reasonably-priced) meal. The sizzling steaks are recommended if you start your tour with lunch here.

After lunch, join the crowds on the pavements of **Jalan Tuanku Abdul Rahman**, the city's longest shopping street and named after the first king of independent Malaysia. Merchandise ranging from textiles and carpets to shoes and leather goods are hawked by both shop and sidewalk vendors. There are also many *kedai makan* or 'eating shops', some of whose food should definitely be sampled.

From the Coliseum Café, head left. One of the first shops is **Minerva Bookstore**, specialising in Islamic literature. Further on, the **Central Shoe Store** has one of largest range of footwear in the city. **Sogo Shopping Centre** on your left is a gigantic mall with a department store, supermarket, bookshop, restaurants, food court and offices.

Tuanku Abdul Rahman
300 m / 330 yds
Itinerary 5
MEDAN TUANKU
Pawagam Odeon
Kompleks Pertama
Jalan Dang Wangi
Kompleks Campbell
Sogo
Jln. Isfahan
Globe Silk Store
Kompleks Wilayah
BANDARAYA
Central Shoe Store
Semua House
Pedestrian Bridge
Lorong Gombak
Eastern Hotel
Minerva Bookstore
Bank Negara KTM Station
Jalan Raja Laut
Jalan Kuching
Coliseum Cafe & Hotel
Grand Paradise
Masjid India Hotel
Champagne Hotel
Jalan Ampang
Bgn PKNS
Lorong Gombak
Jln. Masjid India
Bgn. AIA
Dewan Bandaraya (City Hall)
Dewan Bandaraya Lama (Old City Hall)
Masjid India
Sek. Ren. Keb. St John
Gereja St. Mary
Jalan Tun Perak
Jalan Melaka
Bukit Nanas Recreational Park
Royal Selangor Club
Gereja St John (St John's Cathedral)
Muzium Telekom
Jalan Raja
Dataran Merdeka
Mahkamah Sesyen (Sessions & Magistrates Courts)
MASJID JAMEK
Lebuh Ampang
Jalan Melaka
Masjid Jamek (Jame Mosque)
Jalan Raja Chulan

Age-old Stores

You are now at the junction of Jalan Tuanku Abdul Rahman and Jalan Dang Wangi. Cross the street and backtrack along the opposite side.

One of the country's oldest department stores, **Globe Silk Store**, offers some of the cheapest clothing buys in the city. There are five floors of clothing including batik shirts and the Malay *baju kurung*, (traditional women's wear), textiles, cosmetics and carpets in the Globe, while the top floor has a very nice cafeteria. You may want to take a break with a cold drink and curry puff (pastry with curried vegetables and meat) here.

Top right: fabrics of all colours and des
Right: Jalan Tuanku Abdul Rahman

Further down the street are two more well-established names, the **P Lal Store** and **Chotirmall Store**. There are several textile stores along the way where fabrics and garments from all over Asia are sold. Although prices are generally fixed in the larger department stores, it is possible to bargain at the smaller shops.

Continue down the street and soak in the atmosphere, then turn left into **Jalan Melayu**. On your left are shops that specialise in Indian *sarees* and fabrics. Among them are restaurants that dish up Indian breads and curries. Try a cold yoghurt-based drink called *lassi*, or Indian desserts like the orange-coloured *jelabi*, and *gulab jamun*, a round milk fritter in syrup.

Sarees and Incense

Cross the road into **Jalan Masjid India**, an area of marked Indian-Muslim accent. Running parallel to Jalan Tuanku Abdul Rahman, every available space on Jalan Masjid India is taken up by shops, restaurants and a colourful blend of pavement stalls. The street begins, ironically, with a cluster of Malay shops (**Wisma Yakin**) on your right. The shops sell clothes and food as well as *jamu*, a traditional cure-all medicine made from herbs. Many Malays swear by this stuff, which reportedly also works wonders for the libido. On the left is **Masjid India**, an Indian-Muslim mosque after which the street is named. Although it is only open to Muslim worshippers, stop to appreciate its typically Indian-Muslim architecture. There are also good camera opportunities, but be very discreet and respect the worshippers' right to privacy.

Jalan Masjid India proper is best known for its speciality shops dealing in Indian textiles, Indian ethnic music tapes, ethnic handmade jewellery, religious icons, brassware and other exotica. The road forks in front of the Selangor Mansion; the narrower street on the right is **Medan Bunus**. The broad divider here explodes in a blaze of colour with buckets of freshly-cut blooms and religious garlands displayed on wire enclosures. The flower-

city itineraries

sellers here will thread the blossoms into anything you want, from simple hair adornments to lavish bridal car arrangements.

Continuing down Jalan Masjid India, you will see the budget accommodation-styled Chamtan, Palace and Empire hotels. They are popular with foreign backpackers, not surprising given their colourful ambience, central location and access to cheap, good food.

Jalan Masjid India terminates at a shopping mall called **Semua House** where there is more costume jewellery, clothes and other merchandise. Exit left from Semua House, walk past City One Plaza, turn right at the end of the street and walk through the carpark. From here, be careful not to miss the tiny, almost kitschy, Hindu temple en route. Leave the temple, go left and at Jalan Melayu, turn left and left again into **Jalan Tun Perak**.

Historic Street

Walk down Jalan Tun Perak past the Masjid Jamek LRT Station, next to a monstrous MacDonald's. Turn left into Lebuh Ampang to get to Little India. The area still has a distinctly Indian feel; try a bag of mixed spicy Indian munchies. Several shops deal in Indian-style filigree 22-karat gold. Indian jewellery is traditionally chunkier and more ornate than Western gold jewellery. Behind metallic concertina doors are found Indian *chettiar* money-lending outlets that once ruled the street and indeed, funded many economic activities of locals before World War II.

Continue to the end of the street and turn right into Jalan Gereja then left into Jalan Raja Chulan. At the corner is the restored neo-classical **Muzium Telekom** (open 9.30am–5pm, closed Mon), which charts Malaysia's telecommunications history and features hi-tech displays. The 1928 building used to house a pre-war manual telephone exchange.

For dinner, try **Bijan** (tel: 03-2031 3575) across the road, at 3 Jalan Ceylon. This restaurant serves a variety of classical Malay dishes, including appetisers, salads and curries, amid a contemporary setting. End the meal with a hot dessert or some local cakes.

Above: pavement medicine men along Jalan Masjid India offer traditional massage

6. BUKIT BINTANG *(see map below)*

Browse at the Kompleks Budaya Kraf and a maritime museum; shop and stroll along Jalan Bukit Bintang before tucking into a late-night Chinese porridge supper. This is a half-day itinerary.

Starting point is Kompleks Budaya Kraf on Jalan Conlay, off Jalan Raja Chulan. To get there, take a taxi from the KLCC LRT Station. This tour is recommended as an evening itinerary, but start earlier if you enjoy shopping. You can also use this tour to locate the shops you want to return to later.

This tour is a journey through Kuala Lumpur's mall strip in the city's most prestigious commercial area, the 'Golden Triangle'.

Begin at Jalan Conlay at the **Kompleks Budaya Kraf** (open daily 10am–6pm). This 'one-stop craft centre' – a more upmarket version of the Central Market – showcases quality Malaysian arts and crafts, a souvenir shop, a DIY batik corner, cafétería and the Craft Museum. Souvenir hunters will have a field day here. In one corner of the complex is the Artists' Colony, where many up and coming Malaysian artists can be seen honing their skills. They are generally quite open to a chat, and certainly to purchases.

Head up Jalan Conlay towards Jalan Raja Chulan. On your left, you will see the **Seri Melayu Restaurant** (tel: 03-2145 1833). Behind it on Jalan Raja Chulan is **Chulan Square**, which boasts eight ethnic restaurants.

Just at the junction is the **Muzium MISC** (tel: 03-2273 8088; viewing by appointment only), located on the ground floor. The museum is devoted to maritime exhibits with a good display of model boats, traditional craft, safety equipment and accounts of great maritime explorers. When finished, turn left and head to the busy Jalan Bukit Bintang intersection.

This is the beginning of **Jalan Bukit Bintang**, Kuala Lumpur's most established shopping street, which has been injected with 'mod' thanks to

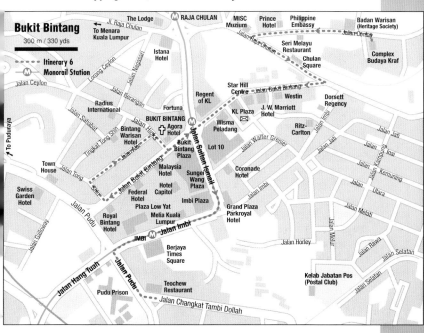

a recent facelift. A wide pedestrian walkway goes all the way up the road, which is lined with open-air cafés, ice-creameries, malls and restaurants. Known as **Bintang Walk**, this is a great place to grub, pub and watch Kuala Lumpur's trendy. The stretch begins at the intersection where you see the trendy **Bintang Shack** fun pub. Further on is the **Westin** and **JW Marriott** hotels. The latter has a good delicatessen and eateries that offer cuisines from all over the world.

Linked to it is **Star Hill Centre**, an upmarket shopping mall that houses exclusive designer boutiques and eateries. The most 'happening' time of the year at Bintang Walk is on New Year's Eve, when the roads are closed and massive crowds throng the area for a free open-air concert, which usually ends with spectacular fireworks.

Coming out of Star Hill Centre, turn left into **Jalan Gading** to browse at shops selling Malaysian couture made from local materials like the *pua kumbu* favoured by the indigenous Iban of Sarawak and the gold *songket* embroidery of the Malays. The clothing is mainly Western style but look out for contemporary versions of traditional Malay and Chinese outfits.

Shops, shops, and more shops

Continuing on along Jalan Bukit Bintang, you come to **Kuala Lumpur Plaza**, a four-storey shopping extravaganza, with the country's largest music store, the American chain Tower Records, as its anchor tenant. If you're feeling thirsty, the broad sidewalk is chock-a-block with open-air cafés such as (another) American chain, Starbucks, and the Sin-gaporean-owned Dome Café; it can be muggy outside, but a cold beer and mist-aided fans do the job in lowering temperatures.

Right next to Kuala Lumpur Plaza is **Lot 10**, a fashionable hangout that has, in addition to upmarket shops and the Japanese-owned Isetan Department Store, numerous chic restaurants and coffee joints where the city's hip crowds like to hang out. There is also a food court in the basement where you can sample street food in air-conditioned comfort. The country's best collection of art, design and architectural publications can be found on Level 3, in Page One. The bookshop also has decent offerings of posters and children's books.

Above: Star Hill Centre
Right: a shopping day at Bukit Bintang

Across the street from the flashy Lot 10 is **Sungei Wang Plaza** and **Bukit Bintang Plaza**, both about 20m (65ft) left of the traffic lights and boasting large department stores. Sungei Wang's anchor tenant is **Parkson Grand**, while the upmarket **Metrojaya** dominates the Bukit Bintang Plaza. The real strength of these stores or, for that matter, most of the stores in this area, is clothing, from *haute couture* designer togs to the more moderately-priced Malaysian-made apparel. In addition, there is no lack of shoes, belts, handbags, wallets and other leather accessories. Metrojaya, Parkson Grand and Isetan also have a good range of imported cosmetics and toiletries. Tip: although cosmetics in Malaysia are duty free, prices at these stores are probably still lower than those found at so-called duty-free stores.

Bukit Bintang's offerings also encompass a whole lot of other goods, from watches and cameras to photographic equipment and books. The prices are reasonable as the area is popular with locals and competition among retailers is stiff. Sungei Wang, in particular, can get very crowded, especially during major festival periods. During the nationwide sales months of July, August and September, goods are marked down by as much as 70 percent, and you get some really good buys then.

Local Eats and a Mega Mall

From Bukit Bintang Plaza, turn left at the main entrance and head down Jalan Bukit Bintang. Keep walking and some 500m (546yds) further down is the **Federal Hotel**. This hotel is as old as Malaysia and was once The Place To Be, where political strategies were devised, and royalty and visiting dignitaries graced the corridors. Today, the revolving restaurant remains popular and the hotel attracts nostalgic guests. Next to it, **BB Park** has restaurants and stalls while **Plaza Low Yat** behind offers PC software, gizmos, food and clothing galore.

For a street food dinner, cross the road to get to Jalan Sahabat and turn right into **Jalan Alor**. Behind placid shopfronts and sanitised fast-food outlets lurks another personality – one that comes out with the stars. The first sign of this is the bright neons and tell-tale red lights that seem to spring up from every second storey window. Jalan Alor transforms itself from a congested city street into brightly lit chaos of food stalls selling a whole range of Chinese cuisine, from the mundane to the exotic – venison, tripe and seafood – for prices beginning at under RM5. Of note are specialities from the northern town of Penang, such as the noodle dishes of *lor mee* and prawn mee, and *lor bak*, deep-fried meat springrolls. At the end of the road at the Jalan Hicks junction, turn right, and you are back in Jalan Bukit Bintang.

Cross the road and turn left until you reach a set of traffic lights. At the junction, turn right and head down **Jalan Sultan Ismail**. Keep to the right side.

Above: Lot 10 is a popular hangout for the hip

At the traffic lights past Sungei Wang Plaza, turn right into Jalan Imbi. You will now be approaching **Imbi Plaza**, which has its back to Sungei Wang Plaza. Imbi Plaza is Kuala Lumpur's computer mall, where you can get bargain basement prices for clones, peripherals and software, including games.

Across from Imbi Plaza, you can literally lose yourself in the megalithic **Berjaya Times Square**. This integrated shopping and entertainment centre has a mind-boggling range of shops, a cineplex, IMAX theatre, bowling alley, indoor theme park, a convention centre, an all-suite hotel and a rooftop park.

Bird's Eye-view

Take a taxi to **Menara Kuala Lumpur** (tel: 03-2020 5444; www.menarakl. com.my; open daily 10am–10pm) for a vertigo-inducing view of the city. An ear-popping super-swift lift delivers you up to the Observation Deck of this 421-m-tall (138-ft) building, which is also known as the KL Tower. This is probably the best place to properly admire the Petronas Twin Towers *(see page 45)*, weather permitting. Menara KL's tower head is inspired by the Malaysian top or *gasing*, while the whole is a combination of

Islamic design and modern technology. The building also has souvenir shops, a revolving restaurant and amphitheatre. Note that queues can be especially long during the school holidays.

Menara KL actually sits on the **Bukit Nanas Forest Reserve**, the country's oldest forest reserve, gazetted in 1906, and the only remaining green lung in the brick-and-mortar clutter of the Golden Triangle. You might want to return here during the day to explore the forest reserve's two short trails. The trails start behind the Malaysian Timber Product Gallery on Jalan Ampang, and wind through shady rainforest.

If you are still feeling peckish, take a taxi back to Jalan Pudu. On the junction of Jalan Pudu and Jalan Imbi is **Pudu Prison**, built in 1895, and once housing the country's most notorious criminals. The prison is now awaiting redevelopment. The mural on its surrounding wall makes up the world's longest painting.

For a Chinese meal with a difference, head for **Restoran Teochew** (tel: 03-2141 4704; open daily 7am–3pm, 6pm–2am) at 270 Jalan Changkat Thambi Dollah, off Jalan Pudu. In this typically noisy Chinese outlet, try Teochew porridge – a plain rice broth – with accompanying dishes such as roast goose, steamed fish and preserved vegetables. Roasting and steaming are hallmarks of this culinary style. Popular *dim sum* is also served from 7am–3pm. Alternatively, head back to Bintang Walk for an endless choice of eats.

Above: Menara Kuala Lumpur (on the left) offers panoramic views of the city

7. KAMPUNG BAHRU *(see map, p44)*

A tour of the oldest Malay settlement; visit a Sikh temple and a mosque; and a browse through a Malay bazaar. This is an easy-going one-hour walk.

Take the LRT to the Sultan Ismail Station; the tour starts from the station. This tour can also be combined with Itinerary 4 (see page 34). Do this tour late on a Saturday evening so you can catch the Pasar Minggu or Sunday Market, which is actually held on Saturday nights.

This tour takes you around the oldest Malay settlement in Kuala Lumpur. **Kampung Bahru** literally translates to 'New Village' in Malay, and has its roots in the early 19th-century influx of Malay settlers to Kuala Lumpur. Though it is not new – the settlement was established in 1899 – this short walk reveals an oasis of rural Malay villages, which has somehow successfully ignored the frenetic urbanisation of its surroundings. This is quite a feat for the area's some 1,000 residents, located as they are on prime commercial land, and considering the pressures they face from government, real estate developers and materialism.

Exit the LRT station, walk down Jalan Sultan Ismail and left into Jalan Tuanku Abdul Rahman, leaving modernity behind when you turn right into **Jalan Raja Alang**. The crowds here spill often over the pavements and onto the road, so look out for traffic. As you walk down Jalan Raja Alang, try some fruit from the stalls on the left. Depending on the season, you might find tropical fruits like durian, mangosteen, rambutan, guava and jackfruit.

One would have thought that a Sikh temple would be out of place in a largely Muslim neighbourhood; but not in Kuala Lumpur. The impressive **Kampung Bahru Sikh Temple** (tel: 03-2144 1800) further down the road is yet another testament to the cultural and religious tolerance practised by Malaysians. The facade of the temple is reminiscent of KL's pre-war shophouses. The gates are normally closed to traffic, but there is a side entrance that allows entry. The temple is open only occasionally and during special festivals, so you may have to make do with a view through the gates.

Above: a Kampung Bahru fruit vendor

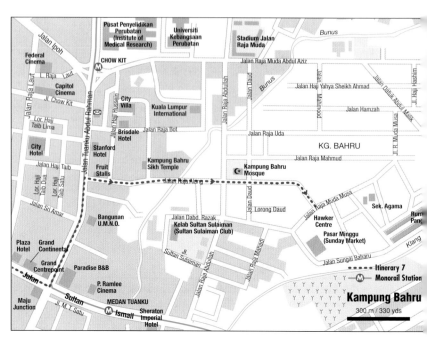

Wooden Charm

Head straight down Jalan Raja Alang till it meets Jalan Raja Abdullah. Just across the crossroads is the **Kampung Bahru Mosque** (tel: 03-2691 3954). Built around 1924, it was one of the first concrete structures erected in the quarter. There are food stalls on either side of the road and itinerant stalls selling Muslim religious paraphernalia. This is one of the places where vendors openly sell Islamic political literature (whose circulation is restricted by the government) by the opposition political party, the fundamentalist Muslim PAS. PAS holds sway in the Malay heartlands of eastern Peninsular Malaysia.

To view traditional houses, have a wander around any of the streets off this road. Typically made of wood, these elevated houses sport Malay architectural features such as the *anjung* or porch for receiving guests, sloping roofs for ventilation, and sometimes, a brick staircase. Often, prayer mats or religious writing grace the doors, underscoring the intense devotion many Muslims have for their religion.

The road ends in a row of shophouses and a mini-bazaar that comes alive on Saturday nights during the **Pasar Minggu** (Sunday Market). Here, you can try authentic Malay foods such as the rice-and-spice *nasi lemak*, rice cakes with coconut gravy called *lontong*, and the East Coast regional favourite of *nasi kerabu*. Alternatively, try a snack of local cakes or *kuih*, often cooked using coconut milk, sticky rice and bananas or a combination of all three.

Because of the area's Malay population, the Muslim Ramadan fasting month *(see page 77)* is a particularly good time to do this tour. Head here just before the break of fast at sunset, when the streets are a riot of food stalls – this is an opportunity to sample delicacies cooked only during this period.

8. Kuala Lumpur City Centre (KLCC) *(see pull-out map)*

Take a snapshot of the world's tallest buildings; sniff around the shops; stroll through the park; and finish with a *latte* by the fountain, a symphony concert or plunge into raucous nightlife at nearby Jalan P Ramlee.

Start at the Suria KLCC, the shopping mall at the base of the Petronas Twin Towers. The LRT runs beneath the KLCC, and the station here is linked underground to the mall. This is a shopping itinerary that can start in the afternoon and end at night, with several suggested options.

The tallest buildings in the world don't seem that impressive when you're up close and personal to them, merely a whole lot of steel and concrete. Then you read the statistics: 65,000sq m (78,000sq yds) of stainless steel cladding, 160,000 cubic m (209,300 cubic yds) of concrete, and let us not forget the 77,000sq m (92,100sq yds) of glass.

The **Petronas Twin Towers** are quite an amazing sight at night, soaring 452m (1,483ft) into a pitch black sky. Full moon nights are particularly mesmerising, and, if you get your vantage point right, the yellow orb appears suspended on imaginary wires between the softly-lit spires.

Completed in 1997, the Twin Towers are the anchor buildings in the 40-ha (100-acre) **Kuala Lumpur City Centre** (KLCC), one of the largest real estate developments in the world. Situated in the former Kuala Lumpur race course, KLCC comprises offices – which are housed in the Twin Towers as well as the surrounding **Maxis** and **Esso** towers; a shopping mall – **Suria KLCC**; a beautiful landscaped park; and a luxury hotel, the **Mandarin Oriental**.

Get a bird's eye-view of all of this halfway up the towers, from the **Skybridge** (open Tue–Sun 10am–12.45pm, 3–4.45pm). This is a 58.4-m (192-ft) double-decked passageway joining both towers at levels 41 and 42. Groups of 20 are allowed entry at 15-minute intervals. You can start queuing up from 8am onwards at the ground-floor information desk (tel: 03-2331 1769) at Tower Two.

Picture Time

For camera buffs, good angles of the Twin Towers can be had from Jalan Ampang and Jalan Tun Razak, as well as from across the lake in the park. Designed by internationally renowned US-based architect Cesar Pelli, the buildings feature local influences such as Islamic designs on the floorplate. In fact, the choice of the number of storeys – 88 – translates in Chinese as 'double luck'.

At the base of the towers sits the mall, **Suria KLCC** (open daily 10am–10pm), a spacious and classy shopping venue with department stores and over 270 speciality shops. Of note are the **Pucuk Rebung Royal Gallery-Museum** and **Aseana**, fea-

Right: the glittering Petronas Twin Towers

turing Southeast Asian handicrafts and products. Have a meal at any of the numerous international eateries, fast-food outlets and food courts. A treat would be a meal in a restaurant overlooking the park, or in one of the cafés that dominate the esplanade front; great for people-watching.

State-owned petroleum corporation, Petronas, which occupies Tower One, has an excellent interactive museum on the oil and gas industry. **Petrosains** (opens daily 9.30am–6pm, closed Mon) sits on the top floor of Suria KLCC.

Evening Options

Once the day cools down a little, explore the lovely **KLCC Park**. Designed by the late Brazilian landscape artist Roberto Burle Marx, the 50-acre (20-ha) garden is artfully laid out, and is great for children, particularly the playground and wading pool. The trees and shrubs in the park comprise mainly indigenous species. About 40 trees have been kept intact throughout the construction and dates to the time when the area was the Selangor Turf Club.

In the grounds is also a *surau,* Muslim prayer hall, featuring a metallic dome and delicate Islamic calligraphy. A jogging track winds around the lake, in the middle of which are fountains and sculptures. The lit 'dancing' fountains in front of the Suria Esplanade are a favourite with locals. There are supposed to be 150 variations to the fountains' 'movements' if you can be bothered to count. Still, they provide great atmosphere for the sidewalk café patrons till well past midnight.

Three options for late-nighters. Movie buffs can catch a movie at one of the 10 cinemas at the top level of Suria KLCC. Culture vultures might opt for a classical or jazz performance at the **Dewan Filharmonik Petronas**, Malaysia's first dedicated classical concert hall. Situated at the podium level and home to the Malaysian Philharmonic Orchestra, this is a small theatre, but it boasts excellent acoustics and an interesting programme. Die-hard party animals would prefer walking to the nearby **Jalan Sultan Ismail/Jalan P Ramlee** nightlife hub where a string of dance and music clubs swing to the early hours of the morning *(see page 74).*

9. BATU CAVES *(see pull-out map)*

This half-day itinerary is a challenging walk up to a limestone cave temple filled with Hindu deities and mythological art.

Batu Caves is about half-an-hour's drive north, or 13km (8 miles) away from the city centre. Take a taxi from town (roughly RM10–15 one way). Alternatively, this attraction features in most outer city tours. Make arrangements with your hotel tour desk (or see pages 90–91).

No visit to Kuala Lumpur is complete without a trip to the Batu Caves, one

of the most sacred Hindu shrines, an intrigue for cave ecologists and geologists, and a popular tourist attraction.

The caves are popular, both with the locals and tourists, for many reasons. Not only is it the southern-most limestone outcrop in the Northern Hemisphere, the labyrinth that makes up **Batu Caves** (open daily 7am–7pm) also supports a variety of exotic wildlife. The main cave holds a shrine of Lord Subramaniam, a deity revered by the Hindus. Every year, at a festival called Thaipusam *(see page 76)*, hundreds of thousands of devotees, watched by a fair share of the curious, converge at the shrine, offering thanksgiving and prayers. Many celebrants offer also acts of penance such as piercing their bodies with sharp spokes, as a sign of their devotion.

For centuries, the caves were obscured by thick jungle, and known only to locals. In 1878, the caves were discovered by American naturalist William Hornaday. The existence of the caves soon became known to the public and the caves became a popular picnic spot for the colonial masters and their wives. During the Japanese Occupation, Batu Caves served as a hideout for anti-Japanese communist guerilla forces. It was only years later that the local Hindu population, with their predilection for sacred caves, began making pilgrimages here to celebrate the Thaipusam festival.

The Climb

The first thing you will notice as you approach the main gates to the temple is the immense concrete staircase that leads up to the temple caves. There are 272 steps in all, making it quite a climb. Monkeys perch in perfect nonchalance along the staircase, and will quite willingly accept bananas (or for that matter, just about anything else). You can buy fruits and nuts to feed the monkeys at food stalls near the row of shops to the right of the staircase. These monkeys are not tame enough to touch though, and a comfortable distance is well advised.

Left: KLCC Park's playground – a delight for children
Top: Batu Caves **Right:** monkeys will greet you along the way

Once inside the main cave, take care to observe religious sensitivities by respecting those praying and keeping a distance from the shrines. Climb down the steps and once back on *terra firma*, you may want to visit the **Gallery of Indian Art**, located to the left of the staircase. Set in another cave, it features intricate clay figurines and paintings from Indian mythological tales. True to the art form, the sculptures of Indian deities and scenes from Indian mythology are painted with bright, sometimes verging on the garish, colours.

There are a couple of souvenir shops, but besides the 'I was at Batu Caves' t-shirts, there is nothing you cannot get in the city. Restaurants serve mainly vegetarian Indian meals at reasonable prices. Wash down your meal with fresh coconut juice served in the nut itself. There isn't much shopping to do but look out for the shop specialising in Indian religious paraphernalia such as oil lamps, camphor holders, incense holders and icons.

If you don't like crowds, avoid visiting at weekends, holidays and Thaipusam, when it's almost impossible to move.

10. FOREST RESEARCH INSTITUTE OF MALAYSIA (FRIM)
(see pull-out map)

Discover a sprawling tropical rainforest located just on the edge of the city. This could be a half-day or full-day tour, depending on whether you enjoy being in the forest.

There are no bus services to this attraction, about 16km (10 miles) from the city, so hire a taxi for the day (RM20–25 per hour; see page 83). The closest KTM Komuter Station is at Kepong where you can catch a taxi for RM15 to FRIM. Arrange with your taxi driver to pick you from the institute later. If you're driving, expect to pay a nominal entry charge for your car. The best time to visit is in the early morning or late evening when the air is freshest and walking in the shady rainforest is relatively cool. Remember to drink lots of water and wear sturdy walking shoes.

The oldest jungles in the world are the tropical rainforests of Southeast Asia and South America. Looking at Kuala Lumpur today though, it is difficult to believe that the city was once covered in dense tropical rainforest. Those who wish to visit an authentic rainforest without travelling too far out of the city need not despair. Tucked away in the hills northwest of Kuala Lumpur is one of the world's oldest forest research centres. Covering some 1,528ha (3,776 acres), the **Forest Research Institute of Malaysia** (FRIM) (open daily 8am–7pm; www.frim.gov.my) showcases the incredible variety of flora and fauna found within a Malaysian tropical lowland forest. Opened in 1926, FRIM has gained increasing popularity among KL-ites and visitors as a peaceful retreat from city living. Once there, finding your way around the well-signposted park is easy. You may wish to pick up maps of the grounds from the public relations

Above: one of Malaysia's myriad butterflies rests on a hibiscus
Right: a canopy of trees at FRIM

office. The nature trails and jungle tracks are shown on these maps, with explanations of the vegetation you can expect to see.

Since this park is dedicated to environmental science research, every attempt has been made to conserve the forest ecosystem. You would notice on your way in that all the signs, buildings and houses are environment-friendly and the structures appear to blend with the surroundings. Traditional wooden houses constructed without the use of nails can also be visited. There is also a museum (open daily 9am–5pm) with informative displays on forestry history and practices in Malaysia, forest products, and research activities conducted by the Institute. FRIM is in fact, positioning itself to be a global leader in tropical forestry research.

One of the most significant features of any tropical forest is its multi-canopied structure, each canopy being a sub-ecosystem in its own right. Unfortunately, this feature is among the first to disappear with encroaching development. In FRIM, the authorities have taken pains to preserve the multi-tiered canopies of the forest.

Mini Showcases

Start with a wander through the various arboretums. There are six of these, showcasing, among others, indigenous fruit trees, conifers, monocotyledenous trees, dipterocarps and non-dipterocarps. Dipterocarps are the largest tree family in Malaysia, covering almost three-quarters of the natural forested areas. The trees in the various arboretums are clearly labelled so that visitors can identify what they see. If you have the time, check out the ethnobotanical garden, a showcase of herbs traditionally used by the indigenous and rural folk. Malaysia shares the same explosive global interest in biotechnology, and this in turn has fuelled much interest in the country's rich repository of traditional medicinal plants.

For trekkers, there are several walks you can choose from. A simple option is to follow the tarred road as it loops through the grounds. Alternatively, you could check out the four short nature trails in the forest. If the public relations office is closed, there is a large map of the trails on the left-hand side of the

road near the administrative blocks.

The **Keruing**, **Salleh** and **Engkabang** trails are fairly flat and make for easy walking. Ranging from 1–1.5km (½–1¼ miles), they would take about 30 minutes to complete. However, the 3km (1¾ miles) **Rover Trail** will get the heart pumping, as it climbs up to **Bukit Nolang** (489m/1,604ft). A real treat would be to tackle the **Canopy Walkway**, used by scientists to study canopy-level flora and fauna. The trail to the walkway is steep but worth the climb for views from the wooden platforms on the walkway. It is open daily 10am–1pm. Entrance is RM5; pay at the Public Relations office (tel: 03-6279 7505; open daily 8am–5pm).

Early mornings and late evenings are when the forest is at its noisiest. A cicada chorus can be accompanied by the sounds of crickets and the numerous calls of birds, which you might just hear if you move quietly and in small enough numbers through the forest. Watch out also for small mammals among the branches such as squirrels and treeshrew, and reptiles such as lizards and skinks sunning themselves on rocks.

There is only one caféteria in the park, so if you're planning a hike, you may want to buy food and drinks there. It is located next to the auditorium. Alternatively, bring a packed lunch and have a picnic in the forest. There is a pretty waterfall which is great for splashing around in. FRIM also offers guided half-day trips starting late morning, which cover the museum, Keruing Trail and Canopy Walkway (RM80 per guide), but you have to book beforehand. To camp overnight, obtain permission from the park authorities first.

11. SUNWAY LAGOON *(see pull-out map)*

Spend a half-day at the Sunway Lagoon theme park; lunch and shop at the Sunway Pyramid Shopping Centre; then take a walk through the Sunway Resort Hotel and the adjacent Pyramid Tower.

Starting point is Sunway Lagoon in Petaling Jaya, about half-an-hour from the city centre. Take the KTM Komuter train to the Subang Jaya Station and then a taxi to the theme park. Works equally well as a morning or after-noon itinerary or even a full-day excursion with the family.

This is a fun-filled itinerary for the entire family while theme park lovers will have a splashing good time. **Sunway Lagoon** (tel: 03-5635 8000; open Mon and Wed–Fri 11am–6pm; weekends and public holidays 10am–6pm; closed on Tues, except during school and public holidays) is Malaysia's best-known and most popular theme park, and part of the Sunway City 'Resort Living within the City' development. Weekends are the busiest days, and December, the busiest month. Although the park can accommodate up to 70,000 visitors a day, it might be a good idea to avoid the peak periods altogether. The entrance fee is RM39 (adults) and RM26 (children) and includes all rides and shows.

Above: a traditional Malay wooden house built without nails at FIRM
Right: Sunway Pyramid Shopping Centre

Fashioned from 324ha (800 acres) of rehabilitated mining and quarrying land, Sunway Lagoon comprises various sections. The **Waters of Africa Park** and **Kalahari Kids** is home to 11 water-rides and the world's largest surf pool, which has huge waves that can rear up to almost 8-m (26-ft) high. You can rent tubes, boogie boards, body boards, surf boards for pools, and lockers to store your personal belongings.

A 48-m (160-ft) long escalator links the Waters of Africa Park to the **Adventure Park** which features seven rides, and a 428-m (1,400-ft) pedestrian suspension bridge across the lake. There is also an indoor games arcade for children. The **Wild Wild West** has seven rides, including the Buffalo Bill Coaster around the 'Grand Canyon', River Rapids, Apache Pots, and the Niagara Falls Flume Ride up a giant rattlesnake and down into a pool.

When you get hungry, there are numerous cafés, restaurants and fast-food outlets. Those who just want to have a look at the park can get quite a nice view from the neighbouring **Sunway Pyramid Shopping Centre**. Fronted by a quirky giant lion's head *a la* the sphynx and 'carvings' of ancient Egyptians pushing shopping carts, this mall has over 300 speciality shops and several department stores. It also has an ice skating rink, a 48-lane bowling centre where the Malaysian national bowling squad practise, and 10 cineplexes. For food, there is a choice of over 40 outlets.

The **Extreme Park** for motorised sports and the **Sunway Petting Zoo**, both of which are located opposite Sunway Medical Centre, provide additional thrills and attractions.

The five-star **Sunway Lagoon Resort Hotel** (tel: 03-7492 8000, www. sunway.com.my/hotel), together with the four-star **Pyramid Tower,** form part of the fully-integrated leisure, entertainment and shopping resort which features more than 1,000 guestrooms, suites, townhouses and villas.

Excursions

T he following excursions are either day trips or overnight excursions to interesting areas outside the confines of the city proper. The tours range from the kitchy (theme parks and a casino in Genting Highlands) to the natural (Kuala Selangor and Fraser's Hill) and the historical (Klang Valley). Also included are two excursions to island communities away from the well-worn tourist paths (indigenous woodcarvers at Pulau Carey and a community of houses built on stilts at Pulau Ketam).

1. PULAU CAREY *(see pull-out map)*

Visit indigenous woodcarvers, have seafood by the estuary, and explore an abandoned capital. Set aside a full day for this tour.

No buses or trains service Pulau Carey, 60km (37 miles) southwest of Kuala Lumpur. Book a taxi (RM20–25 per hour; see page 83) or hire a car for the day. If you drive, head towards Klang, then turn off to Route 5 towards Banting. Turn off at Teluk Panglima Gantang, and this road will bring you across a bridge to the island of Pulau Carey.

Skilled craftsmen are a fast dying breed in Malaysia, although both the Malay and indigenous cultures are rich in traditional creative arts. This itinerary is an opportunity to visit what is probably the Klang Valley's last original indigenous woodcarving village in the heart of an oil palm plantation on **Pulau Carey** (Carey Island).

   Kampung Sungai Bumbon, on Pulau Carey, is home to the MahMeri Orang Asli people, one of the two indigenous tribes in Peninsular Malaysia who are traditional woodcarvers. Like traditional Orang Asli, the MahMeri are animists, in that they worship spirits and conduct ancient ancestral ceremonies. Education and the intrusion of the external world has modernised them, so they speak the official Bahasa Malaysia and wear T-shirts and shorts. Many have also abandoned their woodcarving roots to work in the plantations and in the cities. However, the beauty of their heritage lives on in their work, intricate spirit masks and unique sculptures.

Dream Designs

To the talented, such as head woodcarver Pion anak Bumbon, the designs come in dreams. Others use his work as a base or else refer to a tome on Mah-Meri culture put together by a German researcher several years ago, which painstakingly documents the different types of masks and sculptures in photographs. Amusingly, the book doubles

Left: carving from Pulau Carey
Right: proud woodcarver and his product

as a sales catalogue, for the carvings are also available for sale. And while there is fear of the contamination of commercialism and tourism on the delicate cultures of these people, these might ironically be the only way the Mah-Meri woodcarving tradition can live on.

Still, tourists would do well to respect the chosen lifestyle of these people – though the village is small and basic, it is not poor – and exercise sensitivity when taking photographs. Tourists interested in visiting the village must also seek permission from the Department of Orang Asli Affairs (tel: 03-2161 0577).

There is usually some activity going on at all times in the woodcarving centre in Kampung Sungai Bumbon. Here, masks and sculptures in various stages of completion, as well as craftsmen, sit among the woodchips. All the carvers are men; the women do the finishing. A trademark MahMeri sculpture is the *Moyang Tenong Jerat Harimau*, a monkey and chain ensemble. Moyang is the MahMeri term for spirit, of which there are reputedly over 100.

Jugra Jewels

If you aim to visit the settlement in the late morning, it should be lunchtime by the time you finish. On the mainland side of the bridge, you would have noticed some restaurants on your way in. These would be a good place to cool down with a beer or Coke and have a seafood lunch. Cooked by Chinese chefs, try steamed fish Teochew-style or fried buttered prawns, and a plate of fresh *kailan* (Chinese spinach) cooked in oyster sauce.

After lunch head back to Teluk Panglima Garang, then turn right along Route 5 to head to Jenjarom. Turn at Jenjarom for **Jugra**, an old capital of Selangor. All that is left now of those days of pomp and glory are a graveyard, mosque and palace, now abandoned but still picturesque. The **Royal Mausoleum** is on top of a hill and houses the graves of former rulers. The **Istana Bandar** palace has some European influences, while the minarets and arches of the **Masjid Sultan Alauddin Shah** are testament to the stamp of the Indian-Moorish architectural style.

2. GENTING HIGHLANDS *(see pull-out map)*

Take a journey to the cool hills and enjoy the exhilaration of a highland theme park and casino. A full-day or overnight trip.

There are several ways of getting to Genting Highlands, located 48km (30 miles) from KL. The cheapest is by air-conditioned buses from Puduraya Bus Station. Express buses run every half hour between 7.30am and 7pm (tel: 03-2073 6863); journey time is one hour. The fare is inclusive of the 13-minute cable car ride from the base of the hill to the Genting Highlands Resort at the peak. Taxis (tel: 03-2078 5353) also operate from Puduraya and do free hotel pick-ups within KL (RM55 one way). Travel agents in KL can also arrange packages which include room and transport (see pages 90–91); or else book with Genting Highlands Resort directly (contact details below).

Perched on top of the Titiwangsa mountain range that runs down the centre of the peninsula, **Genting Highlands** is one of Malaysia's most popular recreation destinations. It boasts a family-oriented theme park, the country's largest theatre restaurant and its only legal casino. With other attractions like a golf course, cable cars and amusement parks, and given its close proximity from the city, it is little surprise that the retreat gets very crowded at weekends and school holidays. Located some 2,000m (6,500ft) above sea level, Gentings' midday temperature hovers between 16–23°C (60–72°F), a respite from the city heat.

If spending the night, book accommodation beforehand at **Genting Highlands Resort** (tel: 03-2718 1118; www.genting.com.my) at the peak. The resort comprises seven hotels and apartments, all of which are inter-linked. The resort also owns the **Awana Golf and Country Resort** (tel: 03-6436 9000) located midway up the peak. Besides its golf course, Awana has splendid scenery, jungle treks and waterfalls. A shuttle bus links the Awana to Gentings Highland Resort.

Once at the resort, clear directional signs make it easy to find your way around. If visiting the casino, make sure that you are appropriately dressed. Men are required to wear ties with long-sleeved shirts or a jacket without tie. Alternatively, the traditional Malaysian *batik* shirt is acceptable – these can be rented at the entrance. The casino strictly forbids Muslims from entering, in accordance with the Islamic prohibition against gambling.

Genting's amusement park keeps non-gamblers busy. The outdoor theme park, set around an artificial lake, has rollercoasters, boat rides and a monorail. The indoor theme park has video games, rides and cyberworld activities amid a futuristic setting. There are also three theatres which feature international entertainment such as cabaret dinner shows, musicals and concerts.

Left: Istana Bandar in Jugra
Right: Genting Highlands theme park

3. KLANG VALLEY *(see pull-out map)*

A half-day trip to the richest and fastest-growing area in Malaysia, followed by a seafood dinner in Port Klang.

Get onto the LRT line that ends in Kelana Jaya. From there, hire a taxi for the day (RM20–25 per hour; see page 83). If you choose to skip Shah Alam, take the KTM Komuter service instead from Kuala Lumpur Sentral Station straight to Pelabuhan Klang (Port Klang), 45 km (28 miles) away. Hire a taxi when you arrive. Start this tour in the afternoon and end the day with dinner. Alternatively, combine this trip with a morning tour of Pulau Ketam (see page 58).

This route, which follows roughly parallel to the Klang River, takes you down the **Klang Valley**, the most dynamic and wealthiest industralised region in the country. Kuala Lumpur's first link with the outside world was via a railway line built in 1886. Today, sleek KTM Komuter trains service the route from Port Klang to Rawang in the north. If you are on the LRT, watch out for an archway over the Federal Highway on your right after the University stop. This marks the division between the urban sprawl of KL and its less frenzied satellite town, **Petaling Jaya** (usually abbreviated as PJ),which was originally developed as a low-cost housing scheme in the late 1950s. PJ has since blossomed into a middle-class area of over 500,000 inhabitants who incidentally have the highest rate of personal car ownership in Southeast Asia.

Shah Alam and Klang

From the Kelana Jaya LRT station, hire a taxi and ask the driver to go to **Shah Alam**, the capital of the state of Selangor. Hewn in the 1970s out of rubber plantations, it is one of the country's best planned cities with broad

boulevards and huge roundabouts. Shah Alam's only worthwhile attraction is the **Masjid Sultan Salahuddin Abdul Aziz Shah** (Blue Mosque), the grand Selangor state mosque.

Its distinctive powder-blue dome is one of the most prominent structures in the city – in fact, the dome is bigger than that of London's St Paul's Cathedral. The mosque is laid out along the same lines as the Great Mosque of Mecca and is influenced by contemporary Arabic architecture. To tour the interior of the mosque, remove your footwear, ensure you are appropriately dressed, and make sure it is not the Muslim prayer time.

Tell the taxi-driver to continue to **Klang**, the one-time capital of Selangor. For much of its past, the Bugis, a maritime people from the Celebes Islands (now Indonesia's Sulawesi), played a dominant role in Klang's palace politics. In fact, Klang was one of the three capitals of the state, the other two being Kuala

Left: local girls in school uniform

Langat and Kuala Selangor. As the warlords in each capital set out to establish their hegemony, conflict was inevitable. The 1867 Selangor Civil War was one of the most significant milestones in Klang's history. In the end, it established Klang's dominance as the state capital and, consequently, its development into a major metropolis.

Pre-war Structures

Start your tour at the **Kota Raja Mahadi** on Jalan Kota. It is a fort built by one of the protagonists in the 1867 Civil War. Across the town, along Jalan Tepi Sungai, is **Gedung Raja Abdullah**. It was built in 1856 by Raja Mahadi's opponent, Raja Abdullah, who was key in the founding of Kuala Lumpur through the prospecting of tin. The warehouse, which typifies traditional Malay architecture, has been converted into the **Tin Museum** (tel: 03-559 0050; open 10am–6pm, closed on Fri), bringing back Klang's tin-mining past to life.

On Jalan Timur is the venerable **Sultan Sulaiman Mosque**, built by the British in the 19th century and given to Sultan Sulaiman. It has an interesting blend of British Imperial, Moorish and Arabic architectural styles.

Another building with similar architecture is the **Istana Alam Shah**, the palace of the Sultan of Selangor, located on Jalan Istana. The Sultan no longer resides here but in Shah Alam. However, the palace is still maintained for official functions. It is not open to the public, but is visible some 100m (330ft) to the left (as you face the main gate).

Round off the day with a seafood meal at **Pelabuhan Klang** (Port Klang). About 10km (6 miles) to the west of Klang, this is Malaysia's biggest and busiest port. Tell the taxi driver to take you to the **Bagan Hailam Seafood Restaurant** (tel: 03-3176 2279) in the Bagan Hailam area about 20 minutes away from Klang. There are several restaurants here; head to the one at the very end. Sit on a wooden deck by the Klang River and try its Chinese-style specialties, including baked fish, chilli crab and steamed 'drunken' prawns. Arrange for the taxi to pick you up after the meal and send you back to KL, or drop you off at the train station.

bove: the Blue Mosque (Masjid Sultan Salahuddin Abdul Aziz Shah) at sunset

4. PULAU KETAM *(see pull-out map)*

Relax in a picturesque fishing village and feast on some of Malaysia's wonderful seafood. A half-day would suffice for this tour.

Take the KTM Komuter train from KL Sentral to Pelabuhan Klang (Port Klang), located some 45 km (28 miles) away from KL. Walk to the public jetty and take the 35-minute boat ride to Pulau Ketam island. Ferry services start at 8.45am and operate every 45 minutes. The last ferry leaves the island at 5.30pm on weekdays and 6pm on Sundays and public holidays. Start this tour in the morning and bring a cap and sunscreen lotion as it gets very hot on this treeless isle. You can combine this tour with Excursion 3 (see page 56).

Reputed to be one of the last Chinese fishing villages in the state of Selangor, **Pulau Ketam** (Crab Island) is light years away from Kuala Lumpur in terms of atmosphere. The big city lights and high salaries in KL have enticed many of the island's young people away from the traditional occupations of their forefathers – which till this day centres on the fisheries.

When the island's intrepid pioneers discovered it about a century ago, Pulau Ketam was nothing more than a mangrove mudpile that almost disappeared during high tide. The mangrove stands are, of course, what make

the fisheries here so lucrative. Therefore, instead of looking for greener pastures, the pioneers stayed put, building their houses on stilts. Today, a whole township, complete with pathways, groceries, power station, telephone exchange and bars, all on stilts, has developed on the island.

Everything on the island revolves around fishing: catching it, transporting it to the mainland, or servicing the industry. Because it is so homogenous and relatively isolated, much of the village still comprises traditional Chinese architecture rarely seen elsewhere

Above: stilt houses line Pulau Ketam's banks
Left: canopied street

now, with the family names or famous places of China proudly displayed over the doorways. Concrete is taking over slowly, but wooden houses are still in the majority. Keep an eye out for quaint Chinese temples and altars, which house deities connected with the ocean and fisheries, besides the usual gods of prosperity, wisdom and longevity.

The pace of life is slow, almost as turbid as the mudflats beneath. Watch out for large-clawed crabs and mudskippers in the shallows. Anglers can book to go on boat-based angling trips from either the island or mainland. Island-based tour operators can also bring you to view cage culture farms where fish, crabs and prawns are commercially reared for restaurants on the island and on the mainland.

The town's restaurants serve some of the finest seafood around. Try the **Nam Heng** or **Kim Hor** restaurants near the jetty, both renowned for the island speciality, ie steamed *sembilang* or catfish. The melt-in-your-mouth fishballs and chewy fish-paste noodles are also recommended. The cooking style is of course, Chinese, mainly Cantonese and Teochew variations.

Spending the Night

If you want to spend the night, the **Sea Lion Villa Lodge** (tel: 03-3110 4121) and the **Pulau Ketam Inn** (tel: 03-3110 5206) have rooms with hot water and attached bathrooms. It is best to book beforehand, especially for a chalet on a floating fish farm.

The journey to the island could be tedious as the boat travels through the rather monotonous landscape of mangrove swamps. Cleanliness is also not the islanders' strong point. However, as Pulau Ketam was built to serve the needs of the local community, it is the perfect place to soak in the atmosphere of a traditional Chinese fishing village.

5. KUALA SELANGOR *(see pull-out map)*

A full-day tour (or an overnight for nature lovers) exploring a ruined fortress, a lighthouse and a mausoleum. Go birdwatching in a nature park, enjoy a seafood meal and see the river light up with fireflies.

Hiring a car is the best option; head north on the Kepong-Sungei Buloh-Kuala Selangor trunk road (Route 54) and follow the signs. Alternatively, catch the slow local bus from Puduraya Station for Kuala Selangor, 75 km (43 miles) away. Hiring a taxi from Puduraya will cost RM70 one way for the 90-minute journey, plus RM20–25 for waiting time (see page 83). This excursion is best done in the early afternoon if you want to see the fireflies at Kampung Kuantan in the evening.

Standing at the estuary of the Selangor River, **Kuala Selangor** was once the capital to the Sultanate of Selangor. Back then, the river was a

Right: the Altingsburg Lighthouse

vital means of communication to the otherwise impenetrable interior. The Selangor River was also the key to political and economic power: those who controlled communications along the river also controlled the hinterland. The state of Selangor, in this respect, had three great river systems – the Langat, Klang and Selangor – and the respective nobilities that controlled these rivers constantly bickered for dominance. Ultimately, the group controlling the Klang became pre-eminent. Today, the Klang Valley is the nation's fastest growing urban area, while both Kuala Langat and Kuala Selangor have slipped into obscurity.

What greatness the town of Kuala Selangor once knew remains in the form of ruined fortresses, lighthouses and a mausoleum. Two forts were built to defend the town. The larger and the only one open to the public is **Kota Melawati**, which stands on Bukit Melawati.

From the fort, you can easily walk to other interesting places nearby on the hill, including the Dutch-built **Altingsburg Lighthouse**, which is still functional, and the **Royal Mausoleum**, which enshrines the remains of Selangor's ancient Bugis kings. Other rather gruesome remnants from the old days are a Poisoned Well where traitors to the king were soaked up to their necks in a liquid mixture of latex and itchy bamboo shoots, and a self-explanatory Execution Rock. On weekends, a tram brings visitors up the hill. However, the road around the hill actually makes for a pleasant walk, with huge century-old raintrees and nice lookouts of the surrounds.

Kuala Selangor Nature Park

Walk down the Hundred Steps from the Melawati Gate to the **Kuala Selangor Nature Park** (tel: 03-3289 2294; open daily till late) at the base of the hill. A nominal entry fee helps maintain the park which is operated by the Malaysian Nature Society (MNS). Simple chalet and dormitory accommodation and facilities are available for overnight stays, something which avid birdwatchers would appreciate in order to catch the prolific birdlife feeding at dawn.

Migratory waterbirds are the main attractions here and several bird hides dot the park. Get a copy of the useful bird checklist from the office. Birding field guides are also available for sale there, as well as other wildlife literature and paraphernalia. The best season to spot migratory birds is from September to April when they fly south to Australia to escape the icy weather up north. The park is an important and welcome pitstop for these amazing creatures.

A fairly recent addition to the park is the **Milky Stork Aviary** where a breeding programme of this very rare bird is being carried out with the National Zoo. These storks live only in mangrove and mudflat areas, and it is hoped that the captive-bred creatures will make Kuala Selangor their permanent home when they are released. A good opportunity to learn more about birds is to take part in the MNS bird census (www.mns.org.my) at the park alongside experienced birders.

Above: fine specimen of a Milky Stork

Four trails wind through stands of mangrove and secondary forest and a brackish lake system. Boardwalks provide access to the wildlife. Watch out for bands of Silvered Leaf Monkeys, common Long-tailed Macaques and otters. The mudflats are a good place to catch sight of crabs, mudskippers as well as waders. If you don't feel like walking, rent bicycles at the office, and if there are enough of you, park officers can provide 2-hour nature interpretation tours for a fee. Binoculars are provided. Nearly all the trails are not shaded, so make sure you bring a cap, sunblock and lots of water. Mosquitos are particularly nasty in the evenings, so insect repellent is a must.

There is no food at the park, so head back to Kuala Selangor town, which has a few good seafood restaurants. Specifically, you'd want to go to **Kampung Penambang** (and for this, you will need a car), a fishing village about 20 minutes north of Kuala Selangor. Take your pick of the seafood restaurants lining the main street. Enjoy an early evening meal and then travel to **Kampung Kuantan**, 9km (5½ miles) south of Kuala Selangor. After 8pm, boats take visitors (four people at RM40 per boat) on a 40-minute ride on the river through trees lined with tiny luminescent fireflies. The millions of tiny male beetles flashing synchronously in the dark is an amazing sight indeed. But be sure to avoid rainy nights, as there would then be fewer fireflies to behold.

6. FRASER'S HILL *(see pull-out map)*

Enjoy highland weather and breathtaking views from this hill resort; explore jungle trails and tee off at the picturesque golf course. Set aside a full day for this tour, and preferably stay the night.

Renting a car is the best option. Take the North-South Highway north and turn off at Kuala Kubu Bahru or KKB (100km/60 miles), then follow the signs to go up a narrow and winding road (8km/5 miles) to Fraser's Hill. Alternatively, take one of several bus services from Puduraya to KKB (2 hours), then change buses there for another 90-minute trip up the hill (services going up are at 8am and 12pm; services going down are at 10am and 2pm).

The road from Kuala Kubu Bahru to **Fraser's Hill** (Bukit Fraser) in Selangor is so narrow that a one-way traffic system is in place between 7am and 7pm; odd hours for going up, even for coming down. Outside of those hours, you take your chance with oncoming traffic! It was along this winding road that British High Commissioner Sir Henry Gurney was ambushed and killed by communist guerilas in 1951. If you arrive at the gate too early, have tea at the **Gap Resthouse**, or else drive down to a small but scenic waterfall along

above: picturesque waterfall at Kuala Selangor Nature Park

the main road that leads to the town of **Raub**. There is also accommodation here if you want to spend the night.

An English Air

Fraser's Hill is named after Louis James Fraser, an elusive English adventurer, who had long disappeared when the hill station was built in 1910. He apparently ran a gambling and opium den here for local miners and planters, as well as a mule train.The 1,500-m (5,000-ft) high resort is scattered over seven hills on which sit a series of English greystone bungalows, surrounded by neat English gardens blooming with roses and hollyhocks. The tiny town centre around the clock tower has some rather disastrous newer additions, and there are also high-rise hotels which fail to blend with the landscape.

If you intend to stay the night, a better bet is to go with the economical if run-down state-owned **Fraser's Hill Bungalows and Chalets** (tel: 09-362 2201). Make sure you book beforehand. Other than that, the prettiest and most expensive accommodation is **The Smokehouse Hotel** (tel: 09-362 2226; www.thesmokehouse.com.my), a Tudor concern complete with overstuffed chintz sofas and fireplace – a replica of the original Smokehouse Hotel in Cameron Highlands further north. Even if you don't stay the night here, you mustn't pass up the chance to sample a Devonshire tea or a slice of apple pie in the lovely garden.

From the Smokehouse Hotel, you can walk along the road to **Jeriau Waterfall**, once a pretty picnic spot, but now permanently silted, the result of short-sighted resort development years ago. Alternatively, a shorter route starts diagonally opposite the hotel. The 15-minute **Rompin Trail** takes you to Jalan Sungai Hijau.

Because of its proximity to Kuala Lumpur, Fraser's is crowded at weekends, but there are enough walks and trails to take you away from the madding crowd. The ring road around the 9-hole golf course makes a pleasant two-hour walk, and brings you past the old bungalows and newer resorts. The picturesque golf course is very old. It was carved out of an old tin mine, and is one of the few public courses in the country. You can rent golf sets, trolleys and other accessories here.

Above: pretty English-style gardens surround The Smokehouse Hotel

There are also eight jungle trails of varying lengths, all well-marked and easy to follow, with most being quite easy-going. However, make sure you're wearing sturdy shoes.

The **Abu Suradi Trail** starts at the town center near Puncak Inn and meanders for 20 minutes through forest before crossing the loop road. It then skirts the golf course and ends on the same road that loops back to the town centre. Turn right to return to town, or turn left and walk along the road until you come to the short **Bishop's Trail**, named after the clergyman who, in 1910, went to look for Fraser-gone-missing, failed to find him, and ended up establishing this hill as a retreat.

The most challenging of the trails is the steep 6-km (4-mile) **Pine Hill Trail** which goes up to 1,448m (4,750ft) but rewards the persistent with breath-taking views. The trail brings you through montane habitats: vegetation and wildlife found above heights of 1,200m (3,900ft). As you ascend higher, you'll see the vegetation change from lower montane forest features like trees with buttresses and epiphytes such as orchids, to upper montane forest in the higher elevations, comprising shorter trees, more shrubs and thicker leaves. In contrast, the taller Dipterocarp forests carpet the valleys.

A Bird Watchers' Haven

Here in the Fraser's Hill forests, you'll find some of the richest birdlife in the peninsula, hence the high chance of bumping into groups standing rock-still and peering intently through binoculars. There are an estimated 270 local and migratory species in the forest and this has put Fraser's on the bird-watching map. The activity is promoted particularly through the annual International Bird Race organised by the **Malaysian Nature Society** (www.mns.org.my) together with the Fraser's Hill Development Corporation. This is when teams of birders race to identify the largest number of bird species on the official checklist. Usually held in the middle of the year, this event attracts participants from all over the world.

If you have your own transport, there are a number of good drives around the area, such as the second loop that goes past the holiday bungalows of multinational corporations. The roads are winding, however, so be careful when driving.

Right: tee off in Fraser's Hill

Leisure
Activities

SHOPPING

…ala Lumpur is a shopper's paradise, on par …th Singapore, Hong Kong and Bangkok. …also offers some marvellous opportuni-…s for craft collectors and bargain hunters. …orthwhile finds range from antiques and …ported spices to religious icons and metal-…re. Although the law requires retail out-…s to affix price tags for all goods sold, …rgaining is still an integral part of the …alaysian shopping experience, so you …uld be prepared to haggle. The only …ception would be in department stores and …utiques, where prices are fixed.

…aditional Fabrics

…e would have thought that gold fabric was …reation of Grecian fables. In Malaysia, …wever, it is grounded in reality, and called *…ngket.* Handed down from the courts of …lantan in the Peninsula's east coast, and …tani in Thailand, this cloth is a display …dramatic handwoven tradition featuring …ricate tapestry inlaid with gold and metal-…threads.

Women in some parts of the Peninsula's …st coast still use the traditional two-paddle …or looms to painstakingly interlace …reads, with the best pieces coming from …lantan. *Songket* comes in a multitude …colours that offset the complex tapestry …signs, its richness making it more suit-…le for formal and ceremonial attire. …ngket material can also be turned into stun-…ng jackets, beautiful evening wear and …ractive handbags and shoes.

Batik, the less glamourous cousin of *…ngket,* has more appeal because of its …rsatility, durability and price. In fact, *batik* …chniques have become so popular, they …ve become an art form. Also originally …m the east coast, *batik* is now printed by …ctories all over the country, on fabrics rang-…g from cotton and voile to silk and satin. …tik is used for clothes, accessories, house-…ld and decorative items.

…ft: Star Hill Centre

ght: *songket* – fabric inlaid with gold threads

Silvercraft and Pewterware

Kelantan silvercraft is one of the most suc-cessful cottage industries in Malaysia. It is a craft requiring a great amount of skill, whether in filigree work, where ornamen-tal wire is shaped into delicate tracery, or repousses, where sheet silver is hammered into patterned relief. Kelantan silver is fashioned into a variety of items, from brooches and costume jewellery to serving dishes and tableware.

Kuala Lumpur's own local handicraft, Royal Selangor pewterware, enjoys a world-wide reputation for its stylish and attractive handmade designs. Pewter is an alloy of tin mixed with a little copper and antimony and was introduced to Malaysia from China in the 18th century. The hardness of the metal gives it durability, and its silvery finish does not tarnish. Using traditional methods of casting and soldering, hundreds of items ranging from tableware, candelabra and ornamental pieces to lapel pins, figurines and pendants are crafted.

Kites and Tops

The traditional *wau* and *gasing* (kites and tops), for which the Peninsula's east coast is best known, enjoy both local and inter-national popularity. Both are traditional sports, with kite flying dating back to the 1500s.

The *wau* comes in all shapes and sizes. The most popular and the largest is the *wau bulan* or moon kite, mea-suring 3½m (11½ft) from head to tail and capable of soaring to great heights. Its wood-en frame is covered with stiff parchment deco-rated with designs cut from coloured paper and adorned with colourful streamers. Smaller versions are made as decorative

items. Malaysia Airlines, the national airline, features a stylised *wau* in its logo.

Top spinning is no child's play either, not when the traditional Malay top is about the size of a dinner plate and weighs as much as 5½kg (12lbs). The tops are usually disc shaped, and are carefully balanced for spinning power. A good top in the hands of a skilful player can spin for up to two hours.

Bamboo Products & Beadwork

Cane and wicker are used for furniture and household items. *Mengkuang* (pandanus) leaves are woven into mats, baskets, hats and decorative items, and split bamboo strips are shaped into trays, baskets, food covers and household items.

In Sarawak, *nipah* palm reeds are woven into decorative mats, and rattan is used to make mats and baskets of exceptional durability. A fine quality and well-made mat is said to last up to 30 years.

Beadwork, traditional to the native people of Sabah and Sarawak, is extremely attractive when sewn onto headbands, necklaces, belts, buttons and baskets. Those available for sale in Kuala Lumpur tend to be commercial, but are still attractive souvenirs – at least the designs are native.

Much more rare is the intricate beadwork that typifies the Melaka Peranakan heritage, a blend of Malay and Chinese cultures. This finely crafted work appears on embroidered evening handbags and slippers (*manik-manik*), and feature in select local *haute couture* labels.

Gold

Gold has an allure that transcends international boundaries, but where Malaysian gold jewellery is concerned, there are four major traditions at work here, ie Malay, Western, Chinese and Indian.

Malay, Chinese and Indian goldsmiths tend to use pure gold (up to 24 karat) in fabricating jewellery, as opposed to Western jewellers who combine gold with other precious metals. Even the designs are different. Malay and Indian jewellery tend to have distinct Muslim and Hindu religious overtones, while dragon and phoenix motifs and the use of jade are common features in Chinese jewellery.

The major gold retailers in the city are **Poh Kong Jewellers** in The Mall, **Lee Cheong Jewellers** at Jalan Tun H S Lee, **Habib** at Suria KLCC and Semua House, and international jewellers such as **Selberan** with outlets in Suria KLCC, 1 Utama and Mid Valley Megamall.

Clothing

Good quality cotton, linen and silk, either made locally or imported, are fashioned into ready-to-wear clothing. Most department stores carry their own labels, usually mostly local, and a selection of limited international brands. Most outfits are best suited to warm tropical climes of course, and large sizes can sometimes be difficult to find. However, tailors are equipped to handle made-to-measure orders at fairly reasonable prices and can sometimes deliver within 24 hours.

Where to Buy

The best Malaysian handicrafts, unfortunately, are not found in Kuala Lumpur, but in their home states. A good variety, however, can be found in the **Kompleks Budaya Kraf** on Jalan Conlay, the **Islamic Arts Museum Malaysia** shop and **Central Market**. Pewterware can be purchased in department stores and from **Royal Selangor Pewter** in Setapak Jaya, where there are factory tours too.

There are many shops that sell *batik* and *songket* in Jalan Tun Perak, and it is a good idea to check these out at the **Jalan Tuanku Abdul Rahman** and **Jalan Masjid India** areas, as well as the bazaars in **Kampung Bahru** and **Jalan Raja Laut**.

Shops in **Jalan Masjid India** also sell textiles, religious paraphernalia, metalware and handicrafts from countries such as India, Pakistan, the Middle East and Indonesia.

Chinatown, naturally, is the place for Chinese medicines, herbs, spices and Taoist prayer items. Equally ubiquitous are shops and pavement vendors that stock cheap clothing – albeit with fake brand names – shoes, toys, crockery and other household items. These stalls are also interspersed with pavement vendors from exotic destinations like Nepal and Russia, who sell a range of unusual merchandise. An alternative night market is the one along **Jalan Haji Taib** in Chow Kit.

For better quality and designer labels, the best bet would be the large shopping complexes. Good places to shop include **Lot 10**, **Sungei Wang Plaza**, **Bukit Bintang Plaza**, **Star Hill Centre**, **KL Plaza** and the huge **Berjaya Times Square** in Bukit Bintang; **Plaza Low Yat** and **Imbi Plaza** in the same area for computer and electronics; **Suria KLCC**, **Avenue K**, **Ampang Plaza** and **City Square** along Jalan Ampang; **Sogo** and **Globe Silk Store** on Jalan Tuanku Abdul Rahman and **Pertama Complex** on the same road for leather and budget goods; **The Mall** on Jalan Putra; and **The Weld** on Jalan Raja Chulan. Outside of the town centre, try the **Bangsar Shopping Complex** in Bangsar, the **Mid-Valley MegaMall** close by, **1 Utama** and **Ikano Power Centre** in Bandar Utama and **Jaya's (Section 14)** and **Subang Parade** in Petaling Jaya.

outiques offer exclusive designs that can customised for your requirements. Prices re, however, are generally higher. alaysia has some talented fashion designs, some of whom are doing the country oud internationally, such as New York-ised Zang Toi. Local designer brands are ually available as both *haute couture* and ady-to-wear, and there are some spectacar evening wear collections, some of which ature local influences.

Then there is local dress: for women this mes in the form of the *baju kurung*, the alay long blouse and long skirt outfit, and e *kebaya*, a more body-hugging version f it; the Chinese *cheongsam*; and the Inan *sari* or *salwa khameez* trouser-suit. For en, there is the *baju Melayu*, a cotton or silk tfit with a mandarin-like collar and mpin, a sarong worn around the hips; the hinese Mandarin-collared shirt; and the dian *khurta* cotton top.

Miscellaneous

ameras, pens, watches and mini stereo sysms are relatively inexpensive as they are xempted from import duty. A wide variety f these items is available, and retail outts can be found in all the large shopping omplexes. Imported goods, on the other and, can be expensive. Locally made ather goods are a worthwhile buy. In fact, any leading fashion houses have their roducts made in Malaysia.

eft: an array of *songkok*
above: a Chinatown antique dealer

EATING OUT

Kuala Lumpur is probably not the best place in the world to start dieting. The variety of food is endless, the portions large and the prices reasonable. There is a choice of indigenous Malay, Chinese, Indian and Nyonya food, besides international cuisines like French, Spanish, Italian, Mexican, Korean and Japanese, as well as fusion fare.

With 13 states and culinary specialities within each region, the array of Malay food is almost infinite. As for Chinese food, every provincial variety is available, be it Cantonese, Hokkien, Teochew or Hainanese. Some of the dishes have become so localised they can only be labelled Malaysian, such as *bak-kut-teh*, pork stewed in a soup of five-spice powder and coriander.

Nyonya or Peranakan food is a delicious hybrid of Chinese and Malay cuisines. Indian food covers the spectrum of South Indian, Punjabi, Moghul and Indian-Muslim dishes. There are also different ways of cooking the same foods: seafood, a Malaysian favourite, can be done Chinese or Malay style, while vegetarian food has both Chinese and Indian varieties.

Open-air dining

If the range of cuisines hasn't excited your tastebuds, then perhaps the varied locations in which the food is served might. These range from fine continental restaurants to the street stalls which come alive every evening on most street corners. The quality of the food, however, has nothing to do with where it is served. Some of Kuala Lumpur's best food comes from hawkers and the local know it. Don't fret if some of the stalls do not appear to be clean; just make sure the food is freshly cooked, and avoid ice cubes.

Hawker food is something no visitor should miss while in Kuala Lumpur. Not only do hawkers serve a variety of authentic local dishes, prices are also very reasonable and hawker-stall dining is an experience on its own. Although roadside stalls are a common sight, the modernisation of the city has swept many of these hawkers into the concrete, air-conditioned food arcades of shopping malls.

Open-air hawker centres are scattered all over the city and some of the larger ones are in **Petaling Street** (mostly Chinese food); **Jalan Bunus** (mainly Malay and Indonesian food); **Jalan Alor** (Chinese/Penang food); **Brickfields** (mixed local food but mainly Indian); **Kampung Bahru** (mostly Malay food); **Jalan Imbi** (Chinese Malaysian); **Subang Jaya** (mixed); **SS2** in Petaling Jaya (mixed); and **Damansara Uptown**, **Damansara Utama** in PJ (Malay and Chinese).

Food vendors also group together in shop lots on every other street. Some hawkers keep going till 2 or 3am and there are others who even keep their stalls open till dawn. **Bangsar Baru** stalls are particularly popular among the young crowds returning from a night of partying.

Above: *mee rebus*, Malay-style noodles smothered in spicy gravy

The list on the following pages is by no means exhaustive; entire books have been devoted to the topic. Price categories for a meal for two without drinks are as follows:

$ = under RM30
$$ = RM30–80
$$$ = RM80 and above.

Malay

Kelantan Delights
18/419 Ramlee Mall, Suria KLCC
Tel: 03-2163 4166
Delectable Malay offerings from the Peninsula's east coast, some done with a delicious twist, including chunky beef *rendang* curry, rich chicken rice broth, spicy fish dishes baked, grilled or fried, a variety of fried rice and tasty beef noodles. Portions are generous for the price. $$

Rasa Utara
Bukit Bintang Plaza, Jalan Bukit Bintang
Tel: 03-2141 9246
Specialises in northern Malay cuisine. Try the *ayam percik*, a hot and sour chicken dish which has made the state of Kedah proud. The satay here is also pretty decent, served with generous helpings of thick, spicy peanut sauce, accompanied by rice cakes and sliced onions and cucumber. $$

Seri Melayu
? Jalan Conlay
Tel: 03-2145 1833
Located in a large wooden traditional house, the restaurant serves good Malay food accompanied by a cultural performance. The buffets in particular, are extensive, and definitely value for money, and you get authentic preparations such as *tempoyak* or fermented durian, as well as the healthy Malay salad of *ulam*. $$

Chinese

Golden Phoenix Restaurant
Hotel Equatorial, Jalan Sultan Ismail
Tel: 03-2161 7777
Serves mainly Cantonese cuisine using only the freshest of ingredients. Dishes to try include the sizzling venison on hotplate, braised abalone and salt-baked prawns. A popular venue for corporate dining. $$$

Hai Tien Lo
Pan Pacific Hotel
Tel: 03-4049 4510
Serves excellent Cantonese and Szechuan Chinese cuisine, all *halal* (so that Muslims can eat the food too). Seafood is its specialty, particularly freshwater prawns baked in garlic or fried with noodles. Try also their lamb ribs. Gets busy at lunch so reservations are advised. $$$

Shang Palace
Shangri-La Hotel, Jalan Sultan Ismail
Tel: 03-2032 2388
One of the best Chinese restaurants in the city with good *dim sum* for lunch. It features eight special *dim sum* dishes every month, done in slightly different styles, such as steamed shrimp dumplings with vegetables, vegetarian *siu mai*, and steamed chicken and duck meat in lotus leaf. $$$

Hakka Restaurant
6 Jalan Kia Peng
Tel: 03-2143 1908
Family-owned and run, the cooking here still tastes like it's homemade, from the earthy home-style beancurd to the more exotic braised sea cucumber. The noodles here are also good, especially the fat yellow noodles fried Hakka style, and the finer vermicelli stir-fried with crab. $$

Esquire Kitchen
Level 1, Sungei Wang Plaza Jalan Sultan Ismail
Tel: 03-2148 4506
Dumplings and pork dishes are the main draw of this centrally-located restaurant. The noodle dishes are also commendable, including the *sui kow* or prawn dumpling soup dish with egg noodles, and the Shanghai style noodles. Service might not be great, but the food is always decent. $

Restoran Nam Heong
56, Jalan Sultan (Chinatown)
Tel: 03-2078 5879
Excellent for its Hainanese chicken rice (lunchtime only) and generous portions of local noodle concoctions such as the KL speciality, the dark soy-sauce fried Hokkien mee, and the delicious *wat tan hor* made with flat rice noodles. $

Sakura Café
163 Jalan Imbi
Tel: 03-2148 4315
Besides decent hawker-style meals and a mean Malay *nasi lemak*, (coconut rice with savoury side dishes), try the curry fish head, sour *assam* fish and fried chilly *kung pao* chicken with cashews – all excellent with steamed plain rice. $

South Indian
Devi's Corner Restaurant
69 Jalan Telawi 3, Bangsar Baru
Tel: 03-2282 7591
Roti canai, a fluffy South Indian bread eaten with curry, is served here 24 hours a day; try it plain or with egg, or egg-and-onion variations. Wash it down with a glass of hot *teh tarik*, a frothy hot tea concoction. $

Sri Paandi
254 Jalan Tun Sambanthan, Brickfields
Tel: 03-2274 0464
Curry afficiados will enjoy eating off a banana leaf. Try the excellent fish cutlets, tender mutton curry and spicy chicken *paratel*. Cool down with a choice of plain or fruit-based iced yoghurt drink called *lassi*. $

North Indian
Bombay Palace
388 Jalan Tun Razak
Tel: 03-2145 7220
In a smart bungalow with nice ambience and gracious staff. Try the royal banquet of *tandoori* or vegetarian dishes. There is often live music accompaniment at night. $$$

Taj Restaurant
Crown Princess Hotel, Jalan Tun Razak
Tel: 03-2162 5522

Upmarket establishment and an award-winning North Indian restaurant in KL. Of note is Crab Goa, served in the shell, deep-fried red snapper, and traditional Mulligatawny lentil soup with chicken and rice. $$$

Bangles
270 Jalan Ampang
Tel: 03-4252 4100
One of the city's oldest North Indian restaurants, with kitschy decor – including bangles and mirrors. Try the *kurma*, a light spicy and yoghurt laced concoction in which beef or chicken is stewed. Closed on Sunday. $

Bilal Restaurant
33 Jalan Ampang
Tel: 03-2078 0804
Another very old restaurant – it began as an offshoot of the Federal Bakeries, at one time the city's largest producer of bread. Must tries are the *murtabak* pancake with lamb and onions, honey chicken and prawn curry. $

Vegetarian
Annalakshmi Restaurant
Ground Floor, Mid-Valley Megamall
Tel: 03-2284 3799
Serves a sumptuous buffet spread for lunch and dinner, including breads, excellent *dhal* (lentil) curry, and vegetable dishes The restaurant is beautifully decorated, and you can buy these direct-from-India artefacts next door at their sister concern, Lavanya. $$

Wan Fo Yuan
8 Jalan Panggung, Chinatown
Tel: 03-2078 0952
Good Chinese-style bean curd dishes, centrally located near Petaling Street. Try the crispy mock 'goose', Buddhist mixed vegetables, and greens such as *kai lan*, lettuce or spinach stir-fried with garlic. $

Nyonya
Kapitan's Club
35 Jalan Ampang
Tel: 03-2031 0242
Good Nyonya dishes. Try chicken *kapitan* and Portugese baked fish. Housed in a high-ceilinged pre-war building that has been tastefully renovated. Closed on Sunday. $$

Left: foodstall along Jalan Masjid India

●ld China Café
…l Jalan Balai Polis (Chinatown)
…el: 03-2072 5915

…ot a big selection, but the food is authen-
…c, particularly the chicken *pongteh* and the
…xcellent coconut milk-laced desserts.
…Vhat's best is the ambience: cosy and old-
…vorld. This was in fact a Laundryman's
…ssociation once and now doubles as an
…ntique shop and a restaurant. $$

…op Hak
… Jalan Kia Peng
…el: 03-2142 8611

…A gorgeous old bungalow with excellent
…Nyonya, Malay and Western fusion fare. Try
…he Nyonya set meal which includes *pie tee*,
… savoury pastry, and chicken curry. West-
…rn fare is good as well. Book ahead. $$

…hai

…ama V
… Jalan U Thant, Ampang
…el: 03-2143 2663

…legant setting in the embassy area with
…laborate carvings, lotus ponds and private
…unction rooms. Besides a full menu of
…raditional curries and spicy soups, the tangy
…alads are worth trying. $$$

…marin Heavenly Thai
…evel 2, Centre Court Mid Valley Megamall
…el: 03-2938 3167

…You can't go wrong with the spicy seafood
…om yum soup, the cold *kerabu* salads, and
…xcellent red and green curries (with beef or
…hicken) to go with fried pineapple rice. $

…eafood

…den Seafood Village
…Jalan Raja Chulan
…Tel: 03-2141 4027

…Local seafood as well as imported lobsters,
…oysters and salmon. Most of the food is
…cooked Western style. $$

…u Yu
…14 Jalan Telawi 4, Bangsar Baru
…Tel: 03-2282 0009

…A popular eatery in the midst of the posh
…pub strip, it serves a mean fish head curry and
…buttered prawns as well as good old-fash-
…ioned Cantonese-style stir fried dishes such

as *pai kuat wong* pork ribs, and claypot
dishes with a variety of ingredients. $$

Lobsterman
18 Jalan Delima, off Jalan Imbi
Tel: 03-2141 6772

This restaurant dedicated to fresh seafood
offers shellfish, crustaceans and fish to
delight the plate. $$

Japanese

Chikuyo-tei
2/F Hotel Istana
Tel: 03-2141 4328

Quality food and value-for-money set meals.
Recommended is their Chikuyo-zen, a set
dinner with starter, vegetables, soup,
shashimi, tempura, unagi (eel) and fruit. $$$

Kampachi
Equatorial Hotel, Jalan Sultan Ismail
Tel: 03-2161 7777

Known for the quality and freshness of its
food. Of note are its sashimi and grilled
teriyaki beef or chicken. $$$

Wasabi Bistro
Mandarin Oriental Hotel, KLCC
Tel: 03-2163 0968

The cuisine is Pacific Rim-inspired Japanese
fusion. House specialities include the papaya
motoyaki, seafood with hollandaise sauce and
chunks of papaya, and dynamite roll of spicy
tuna and crab. Bookings are essential. $$$

Above: cheap chillies

Western

Ciao
428 Jalan Tun Razak (near RHB Bank)
Tel: 03-9285 4827
Excellent Italian pasta and pizza in a lovely bungalow setting. What is good value is the set lunch comprising appetizer, main meal, dessert and coffee. Night time sees the candles and soft music set a romantic tone. $$$

Frangipani
25 Changkat Bukit Bintang
Tel: 03-2144 3001
The restaurant is as much a showstopper as the food. Converted from an old bungalow, the chic setting is the perfect foil for its modern French cuisine. Start with drinks at the bar upstairs before stepping into the restaurant on the ground level. Open for dinner only Tues to Sun. $$$

Oggi
Regent Kuala Lumpur
160 Jalan Bukit Bintang
Tel: 03-2141 0661
Willowy gauze curtains and dramatic pillars set the stage for this restaurant specialising in Italian fare. High-quality ingredients go into the making of its pastas and pizzas and also the meat and seafood entrees. $$$

Chalet Restaurant
Equatorial Hotel, Jalan Sultan Ismail
Tel: 03-2161 7777

Enjoy European cuisine in Swiss-styl ambience for lunch and dinner – fres salads, grilled meats, fondue and a goo selection of fine wines. $$

Coliseum Café
98 Jalan Tuanku Abdul Rahman
Tel: 03-2692 6270
A historical landmark with loads of atmo sphere, this place is best known for its siz zling steaks and baked crab house specialty End with the wicked banana and chocolat spring roll with ice cream. $$

Hard Rock Café
Wisma Concorde
Jalan Sultan Ismail
Tel: 03-2144 4062
Tested formula: rock memorabilia, lou music and American food. Popular are th *fajitas* and huge BBQ beef ribs. End with sinful ice cream-topped choc brownie. $$

La Bodega Tapas Y Vinos
16 Jalan Telawi 2, Bangsar Baru
Tel: 03-2287 8318
There's nothing like Spanish *tapas* and col *sangria* on a hot KL night here where the tables spill out onto the Bangsar sidewalk Alternatively, order the cheese platter to g with the South American wines on the list $$

L'Opera
Ground Floor, Wisma Peladang,
Jalan Bukit Bintang
Tel: 03-2144 7808
This commands a great *al fresco* dining location in Bintang Walk. It has a lovely range of authentic Italian food including freshly prepared pastas, pizzas galore, traditional desserts and coffees. $$

JW Marriott Gourmet
Lower Ground Floor, Star Hill Centre
Jalan Bukit Bintang
Tel: 03-2715 9000
Sandwiches, quiches, salads and pastas – this gourmet deli serves a nice range of ligh lunches. Have a freshly baked pastry or a slice of cake with your tea or coffee, or quaff a glass of wine as you people-watch here. $

Above: sidewalk dining at La Bodega in Bangsar
Right: night market scene at Jalan Petaling

NIGHTLIFE

[Ku]ala Lumpur's nightlife is not as racy as [M]anila's or Bangkok's but there is still plenty [of] action for visitors who want to see a dif[fe]rent side to the city. Known as the 'gar[de]n city of lights', Kuala Lumpur lives up to [its] name when the sun goes down.

The city has a varied nightlife, with many [sh]ops open until 10pm, and an active [str]eetlife as well. Whether it is eating and [sh]opping, night-clubbing or pub crawling, [th]ere is enough to keep you awake till the [sm]all hours of the morning.

[N]ight Markets

[E]very day, the city authorities close off a [st]reet or two to vehicles, turning the space [ov]er to small-time traders and hawkers for [th]e evening. The *pasar malam*, or night mar[ke]t, is a hallowed institution in Malaysia. [T]hese are colourful and lively open-air [ba]zaars whose itinerant vendors sell every[th]ing from fresh vegetables, meat, fish, fruits [an]d cooked food, to toys, household ware, [el]ectronics, clothes and bric-a-brac.

However, it is not just the variety of mer[ch]andise that makes the night markets special [fo]r KL-ites. The markets are social institu[ti]ons as well, providing an opportunity for [ne]ighbours and friends to meet in the cool of [th]e evening. Since night markets are not nec[es]sarily set up in the same spots every evening, [as]k your hotel concierge for specific loca[ti]ons each evening. This information can also be obtained from the Tourist Information Centres *(see page 90)*. Popular night market sites are **Jalan Berhala** and **Brickfields** on Thursday, and **Jalan Telawi**, **Bangsar** and **Taman Tun Dr Ismail** on Sunday.

Lounges

Lounges are found in hotels and are often places where business deals are sealed over drinks or coffee. Lounges are also hot favourites with the older crowd and snuggling couples. Open in concept and furnished with comfortable sofas, the entertainment usually comprises easy listening music by a live band, more often than not Filipino, or a singer and pianist. One of the most popular and lively lounges is at the **Concorde Hotel** in Jalan Sultan Ismail; one of the most posh is at the **Shangri-la Hotel**, across the road.

Dance Clubs

There are quite a few dance clubs in Kuala Lumpur, ranging from the ultra-trendy where yuppies come dressed to kill, to dark seedy bars that you wouldn't want to be caught dead in. Most good hotels have dance clubs as standard fixtures. Most are open on weekdays from 5pm–1am, with happy hours ending at around 9pm; on weekends these clubs remain open till 3am or later.

House music is pretty hot, with foreign DJs doing the circuit. Some clubs throw in a little R&B and top 40s to keep the crowd happy. Places to party include **Qba** at the

Westin KL hotel; **Hard Rock Café** at the Concorde Hotel; **O*range** at Jalan Kia Peng; and **The Backroom** behind Shangri-La Hotel. Central Market's Annexe hosts the **The Disco** (formerly a cinema) and the **Liquid Club**, popular with KL's gay community.

Huge multi-entertainment complexes seem *de regiuer* in the Golden Triangle club cluster at **Jalan Sultan Ismail/Jalan P Ramlee**. Here, each complex comprises several restaurants and bars, and even different dance areas. Among these megaliths are **Espanda**, **Beach Club**, **Nouvo**, **TwelveSI**, and **The Grand Modestos**. Nearby at Jalan Ampang is **Zouk Club**, a hip place with live bands.

Meanwhile, in the traditional publand of **Bangsar Baru** *(see also page 33)*, tiny dance places are springing up all the time. In **Petaling Jaya**, head for hot spots like **Viva** at the Eastin Hotel in Jalan Damansara, and **Uncle Chilli's** at the PJ Hilton. At the **Sri Hartamas** area, you will find **The Orange** for jazz and R&B music, along with dance club **Bar Med**.

This list is by no means exhaustive. Daily newspapers carry comprehensive listings of entertainment spots around the city.

Pubs

While alcohol is not a central feature of traditional Malaysian culture, an increasing number of office workers, businessmen and executives congregate at these watering holes after work to wash down their tribu-lations with a beer or two before trudgir home. Most pubs serve food, the mainsta being sandwiches, fried chicken wings ar French fries. In addition, many pubs featur live music and almost all have soun systems, playing popular tunes.

Besides the Golden Triangle are **Bintang Walk** has become *the* place to catc the best 'happy hour' prices. Among th numerous restaurants, **Shook!** and **Cesar Bistro** (both in Starhill Centre) stand o for ambience and variety whilst **Havan Club** (JW Marriott Hotel) has the strongho on wine and cigars. The **Asian Heritag Row** at Jalan Doraisamy has two hangout Blonda and Bar Savanh.

The suburbs remain the strongholds f pubbing. In **Bangsar Baru** *(see also pag 33)*, **Canteena's**, **Ronnie Q's**, **Alexis** an **Finnegan's Irish Pub** are but a few of th spots that blend outdoor chic with urba cool. In the **Sri Hartamas** area, **Soule Out**'s outdoor beer garden keeps it up the in the watering hole trend-meter, alongsid **Finnegan's** and **Bistro 1957**.

Karaoke Lounges

Kuala Lumpur's – indeed, the country's greatest nighttime passion is karaoke Karaoke lounges here are essentially spruce up bars equipped with audio facilities tha project musical lyrics and a suitable them on a TV console while playing the instru mental background through a sophisticate hi-fi set-up.

Above: nightlife along Jalan P Ramlee

The better karaoke lounges include the ...gh-end **Club de Macao I** at the Rennai-...nce Hotel, **Las Vegas** on Jalan Imbi, and ...d Box at Plaza Low Yat, off Jalan Bukit ...ntang, and Sunway Pyramid.

Many restaurants also offer karaoke fa-...ities, just as there are discos with karaoke ...oms, such as **Uncle Chillie's** in the PJ ...lton, and the Hotel Istana's **Musictheque**.

...ve Music

...though Malaysians are generally musi-...lly inclined, finding places that play good ...ve music can be difficult. The few good ...ots that have bands normally feature cover ...rsions of popular hits. Although most of ...e places listed below feature live acts, it ...wise to call ahead and check. When no ...nds are in attendance, the same places have ...ejays playing the latest dance music.

Planet Hollywood at Bintang Walk, ...ard Rock Café in the Concorde Hotel, ...he Emporium and Beach Club along ...lan P Ramlee, and Uncle Chilli's in PJ ...lton sometimes feature live groups. **Blue ...loon** in Equatorial Hotel has a band that ...ays oldies but goodies from the 1950s, ...hile bands in Kit Kat Lounge at the ...heraton Imperial Hotel do requests dating ...om the last 40 years. Many other leading ...otels in KL also have live music in their ...ar lounges and discos every evening. Live ...zz may also be sampled at **The Jazz Bar** ...O*range club in Jalan Kia Peng.

For canto-pop (Chinese-language hits ...om Hong Kong and Taiwan), head for ...ow Wow Café on Jalan Balai Polis in ...hinatown. Catering to an almost exclu-...vely young Chinese crowd, this is where ...combination of pop star wanna-be's and ...ig names belt it out nightly.

...heatre and Dance

...here is a small but active theatre scene in ...uala Lumpur, with plays held infrequently ...t **Dewan KR Soma** at Wisma Tun ...ambanthan, off Jalan Tun Sambanthan, and ...stana Budaya, the massive national theatre. ...he only venue that features regular acts is ...he Actor's Studio in Bangsar. It features ...rofessional and amateur performances ...nainly in English, but sometimes in Bahasa ...Malaysia and Mandarin. These include

revue, modern dance, stand-up comedy and skits. There is a lot of interest in Malaysian artforms, whether it be localising foreign works, or the incorporation of Malay, Chinese or Indian elements in original productions. The results vary, but can be interesting. For details, check the dailies or with The Actor's Studio, tel: 03-2094 0400, website: www.theactorsstudio.com.my.

Three other professional groups to watch out for are classical Chinese orchestra, **Dama**, and classical Indian dance exponents **Sutra Dance Theatre** and the **Temple of Fine Arts**, which stages large-scale productions.

Cultural shows are held on weekends, and Tuesdays and Thursdays at 3pm at the MTC (RM5). Some restaurants also feature local dance performances of the commercial variety. Among them is **Seri Melayu** in Jalan Conlay and **Saloma Bistro** at the MTC, during their nightly dinner buffet.

Classical Music

The top classical concert venue in Kuala Lumpur is the **Dewan Filharmonik Petronas** concert hall in the KLCC (tel: 03-2051 7007, 10am–6pm, closed on Sunday, www.dfpmpo.com). There is a full and interesting programme of performances by the resident Malaysian Philharmonic Orchestra (MPO) throughout the year. For the current season's concert programme, check out the orchestra's internet homepage at www.malaysianphilharmonic.com. Guest artistes occasionally appear with the orchestra, and the Petronas Dance Troupe sometimes perform as well.

Right: designer shades

CALENDAR OF EVENTS

The multi-ethnic mix in Malaysia – a blend of Malays, Chinese, Indians, Eurasians and at least 30 other indigenous and ethnic groups – weaves a social fabric embroidered with tradition, variety and colour. Auspicious occasions and festivals of religious and cultural significance of each group take place throughout the year, in consonance with different calendar systems.

Malaysians observe an 'open house' tradition during these festivities, inviting friends and relatives to their homes for social visits and to indulge in that great Malaysian pastime – eating.

A good many festival dates are not fixed as they shift annually, depending on the lunar and Muslim calendars. Check with Tourist Information Centres (*see page 90*) for the exact dates of celebrations.

January/February

Thaipusam (January/February): Commemorates the handing over of the *vale* (trident) of virtue to the Hindu deity, Lord Subramaniam. It is celebrated by Hindus all over the country with great fervour. Thousands converge at one of the holiest Hindu shrines at Batu Caves to offer thanks and prayers, many of them bearing *kavadi*, a wooden framed structure designed to carry containers of milk and rose water, as offerings. Sometimes the procession takes on a macabre dimension, with skewers pierced into the bodies of the *kavadi* bearers. The crowds start gathering the evening befo when the statue of Lord Subramaniam drawn by chariot from the Sri Mahama amman Temple at Jalan Bandar to the te ple cave. *Kavadi*-bearers generally beg their 272-step climb at dawn, but devote throng the temple the whole day.

Federal Territory Day (February Kuala Lumpur brings out the firework streamers and balloons to celebrate its birt day. Special events, from cultural and m sical performances to watersports, take pla throughout the day.

Chinese New Year (January/February This important Chinese festival heralds t first moon of the lunar new year, and marked by prayers, reunion dinners and lic dances. Although only two days are desig nated as public holidays, most Chines owned shops close for up to five day Chinatown is at its best before the celebr tion. Join the crowds in their last-minu shopping on the eve at Jalan Petaling ar try the festive goodies, many of which a imported from China.

May/June

Colours of Malaysia (May/June): Month long nationwide fete of festivals, food ar handicrafts held in hotels and large malls; i Kuala Lumpur, different venues host diffe ent regional themes.

Wesak Day (May/June): The most signifi cant festival for Buddhists commemorate the birth, enlightenment and death of Lor Buddha. Temples are packed with devotee offering prayers and giving alms to th monks. Visit the International Buddhist Pa goda along Jalan Berhala, Brickfields, c the temple off Jalan Gasing in Petaling Jay The air is usually thick with the smell an smoke from giant joss-sticks on the templ grounds, compounded by that from the hun dreds of joss-sticks raised in prayer by con stant streams of devotees to the statue o Lord Buddha and other deities. Worship pers receive yellow strings from the monk to be worn around their wrists for luck.

August

National Day (August 31): Malaysia's Har Kebangsaan is celebrated with a mammoth parade at Dataran Merdeka along Jalan Raja

Left: Chinese New Year festivities

with processions of floats representing all the states. Here, in 1957, the declaration of independence was made. The parade starts early at around 7 or 8am, and is difficult to view unless you go to the square very early. Alternatively, watch it on TV. Roads in the immediate vicinity are closed to traffic.

September

Mooncake or **Lantern Festival** (September): This is a Chinese festival to celebrate the overthrowing of the Mongolian Dynasty by the people in China. Messages hidden in specially baked mooncakes were supposed to have helped fuel the revolution. Traditionally filled with sesame seed paste and egg, modern moon cakes now have a variety of fillings, including green *pandan* (screwpine leaves) and even the stinky durian fruit. In the evening, children play with festive lanterns while women pray to the Goddess of the Moon.

Festival of the Hungry Ghosts (September): Altars with tiny teacups and food as well as candles on street corners and pavements are the most visible signs of this Chinese celebration. The Chinese believe that during this seventh month of the lunar calendar, the gates of hell open and souls in purgatory wander the earth, and must therefore be appeased with the offering of food. Joss sticks and 'hell money' are sometimes burned. This is believed to be an unlucky month to get married or move homes.

October/November

Deepavali (October/November): Also known as the Festival of Lights, this falls in the Tamil month of Aipassi. Hindus celebrate the triumph of light over darkness and good over evil with prayers, and line their gardens with oil lamps to receive blessings from Lakshmi, the Goddess of Wealth. Another 'open house' affair.

December

Christmas (December 25) is celebrated with imitation fir trees, carolling in shopping malls, and midnight masses in churches. Shopping complexes and hotels take the lead with their decorations, complete with sleighs.

Variable Dates

Hari Raya Puasa: Celebrates the first day of the Muslim month of Shawal, following a month of strict fasting and prayers known as Ramadan. The start of the fasting period is governed by the Muslim calendar. Muslims usher in Hari Raya Puasa by attending prayers, followed with 'open house' the whole day long, for guests to feast on delicious homecooked Malay food, cakes and cookies.

Hari Raya Haji, a Muslim festival celebrating the *haj* or religious pilgrimage to Mecca. This is a quieter affair than Hari Raya Puasa, with prayers, and the slaughtering of cows and sheep. **Maal Hijrah** is the Mulsim New Year, another sober religious celebration at mosques. Quran recitals are also held.

Above: Thaipusam devotee at Batu Caves

Practical Information

GETTING THERE

By Rail

The main train line from Singapore to Bangkok and beyond stops at the **Kuala Lumpur Sentral Station** (Stesen Sentral Kuala Lumpur). The **KTM Berhad** trains are modern and the service is efficient. Travellers generally take the express services, which are faster because they make a minimal number of stops. There are three classes of service. Most trains are air-conditioned and have buffet cars serving simple meals. Videos keep most passengers entertained but can be disturbing to those who want to sleep, read or simply enjoy the scenery. Sleeping berths are available on long distance trains. These are a comfortable and cheap source of accommodation for those on a budget.

There are day and night trains to both Singapore and Butterworth in Penang. From Butterworth, there are train connections to the north into Thailand. For more information, call 03-2267 1200.

Several times weekly, the luxurious rail service **Eastern & Oriental Express** makes a brief, late night stop at the Railway Station. The cream-and-green coloured (and very expensive) trains carry up to 130 passengers from Singapore to Kuala Lumpur and Butterworth, terminating in Bangkok (and vice versa). Passengers may embark at any of these points. For reservations and more information call its Singapore office, tel: 65-6392 3500; www: orient-express.com.

By Sea

Kuala Lumpur's closest seaport is **Port Klang** (Pelabuhan Klang), about 40km (25 miles) away, and linked to it by highways, buses and the KTM Komuter train service. Ferries from Sumatra, Indonesia, dock here; smaller ferries travel daily here from Tanjong Balai near Medan. Port Klang is the main port of call for regional cruise ships, and less regularly, the international liners.

By Road

The North-South highway from Singapore to the Thai border provides a convenient means of travel through Peninsular Malaysia, the entire trip taking about 12 hours by car one way. There are two links from Singapore: across the Causeway from Woodlands to Johor Bahru, and Linke Dua (Second Link) from Tuas to Tanjung Kupang. Try and avoid crossing the border on Friday afternoons and during public holidays because of the traffic congestion at the checkpoints.

Long distance buses and taxis also travel to and from Kuala Lumpur to most destinations on the peninsula as well as Singapore and Thailand. The main interstate bus stations are at **Puduraya** (tel: 03-2070 0145) near Chinatown, and **Perhention Putra** (tel: 03-4043 8984) near The Mall. The air-conditioned express buses are fast and comfortable, with video entertainment on board. The buses make occasional stops for drinks, meals and toilet breaks.

Plusliner (tel: 03-2272 1586; www.plusliner.com), which picks and drops passengers at the old Kuala Lumpur Railway Station, operates daily coach services to various cities in the peninsula as well as a direct service (4 hours) to Singapore on its executive NiCE coach service with only 26 seats.

Long distance air-conditioned taxis also leave from Puduraya. Share the cost with three other passengers to save on cost or book the entire taxi.

Left: KL Railway Station at night
Right: North-South Highway

By Air

The **Kuala Lumpur International Airport** (KLIA; www.klia.com.my) is located 70km (43 miles) south of the city in Sepang and is one of Asia's biggest and most modern airports. Planes arrive and depart from four satellite arms, which are linked to the main terminal building via an aerotrain.

KLIA houses the country's national carrier **Malaysia Airlines** (MAS) (tel: 03-7846 3000, www.malaysiaairlines.com.my) which provides both international and domestic connections to destinations on the peninsula and east Malaysia.

MAS has discounted fares on some domestic flights but this means travelling at inconvenient times. If interested, ask for its special 'night tourist fares'.

The cheapest domestic flights are on **Air Asia** (tel: 03-7845 7777, www.airasia.com). Occasionally, Internet bookings get you rates even lower than train fares! Its flights and destinations are limited but the airline is quickly expanding, including regionally.

Another small airline, **Berjaya Air** (tel: 03-7847 6828, www.berjaya-air.com), flies to places like Melaka, Tioman, Pangkor and regionally to Koh Samui in Thailand, Padang in Indonesia and Singapore.

Kuala Lumpur is reputed to be a good place to buy cheap international fares. In addition to MAS, Kuala Lumpur is also well-connected by international carriers.

Departure tax on international flights is RM40 while that of domestic flights is RM10. Tickets purchased in Malaysia will include the tax, while those purchased outside the country, probably will not. If so, you may pay the tax at the check-in counter.

Arriving in Kuala Lumpur on an international flight is easy, with all signs in both Bahasa Malaysia and English.

Airport Transfers

For the **airport limousine** service, buy a coupon with fixed fares (RM67: budget, RM92: premier) for destinations in the city centre, but this is expensive if you're alone.

Express coaches (tel: 03-6203 3067) depart from the basement every 30 minutes (from 6.15–12.30am) to Hentian Duta, and makes drop-offs at major hotels (RM20). Other buses go to the Star LRT Station at Jalan Chan Sow Lin, or to Nilai, south of KL.

The fastest way to the city centre is the high-speed **KLIA Express train** whi takes 28 minutes to get to KL Sentral Stati (RM35). If you are flying with Malaysia A lines for the return trip, you can do a flig check-in, including luggage, at the Centr Air Terminal (CAT) at KL Sentral.

Accommodation and car hire faciliti are also available at the airport. City tax cannot legally pick up passengers at the a port, but you can catch any taxi from t city to the airport – the fare is based o mileage plus a surcharge.

TRAVEL ESSENTIALS

When to Visit

Kuala Lumpur is hot and humid. Daytim temperatures can reach a high of 33°C (91° while the nights can be balmy, with the tem perature dropping by as much as 10°C although most times, the difference is sligh Humidity is almost always above 80 pe cent. As the city has no defined seasona weather patterns, a visit can be planned fo any time of the year. The central mountai range keeps out the worst of the north-ea monsoon (November–February), and th city's inland location protects it from th south-west monsoon (July–September).

Kuala Lumpur gets its share of heavy rai though, with downpours and flash flood mostly in the afternoon and early evening

Visas

Visa requirements change, so check wit the relevant Malaysian embassy/consulat before travelling. At time of press, citizen of the Commonwealth and ASEAN, Irelan Switzerland, the Netherlands, San Marin and Liechtenstein do not need a visa to visi

The following nationals do not need visa for a visit not exceeding three months Austria, Australia, Belgium, Italy, Japan South Korea, Tunisia, the United States Germany, France, Norway, Sweden, Den mark, Belgium, Finland, Luxembourg an Iceland. Citizens of Bulgaria, Rumania, Rus sia (CIS) and Yugoslavia are allowed a seven day visa-free visit.

Immigration requests that travellers hav

ssports that are valid for at least six months time of entry.

Tourist visas may be extended by applying at the **Immigration Department**, Block . Pusat Bandar Damansara, Damansara eights (tel: 03-2095 5077; Monday–Friday am–4.15pm, second and fourth Saturday am–12.45pm).

accinations

. yellow fever vaccination is required if arriving from an infected country.

lothing

lothes should be light and loose so pack ottons and natural fibres, instead of synetics. Sunglasses, sun block and umbrellas re advisable. Shoes should be removed before entering temples and homes, so slipns are handy.

lectricity

ower supply is 220 or 240 volts at 50 Hz ycle. Most outlets use the three-pin, flatronged plugs and many hotels have 110-olt shaving sockets.

ime Differences

Kuala Lumpur is 8 hours ahead of GMT and 6 hours ahead of US Pacific Standard Time.

GETTING ACQUAINTED

Geography and Population

Malaysia's land mass of 330,434sq km 127,580sq miles) covers the Malay Peninula and a third of Borneo. About half the country is still under virgin tropical rainforst cover, encompassing numerous species-ich ecosystems that have earned Malaysia its status as one of 12 mega-biodiversity centres in the world. About 20 percent more of its land area comprise plantations, mainly oil palm and rice fields.

Kuala Lumpur, the nation's capital, is situated about halfway down the west coast of the peninsula and 35km (22 miles) inland. Dubbed Malaysia's Garden City of Lights, it sits at the confluence of the Klang and Gombak rivers and is a metropolis with an area of about 234sq km (90sq miles) populated by over 2 million inhabitants.

Malaysia's 25-million population comprises mostly indigenous Malays, Dayaks, Muruts, Bidayuhs, Kadazans, Orang Asli and about 30 other cultures of Melano-Polynesian stock (making up 60 percent of the population), followed by substantial numbers of Chinese and Indians as well as smaller numbers of Portuguese, Eurasians and others. The Chinese largely belong to the Cantonese, Hokkien and Hakka dialect groups. The Indians consist mainly of Tamils, followed by significant numbers of Malayalis, Punjabis and Sindhis.

Government and Economy

As an ex-British colony, Malaysia's legal and economic systems trace their origins to England. Although the sultan of each state still plays a role within the country, this role is largely ceremonial. The political system is a constitutional monarchy with the King, or the Yang di-Pertuan Agung, elected every five years on a rotational basis by the 11 peninsular state rulers.

Malaysia comprises 13 states located on the peninsula along with Sarawak and Sabah in East Malaysia on the island of Borneo. In addition, there are Federal Territories comprising the administrative capital of Putrajaya, Kuala Lumpur and the international offshore financial centre of Labuan.

There are two houses of parliament; the lower house or Dewan Rakyat, and the senate or Dewan Negara. Some of the latter are appointed by the Yang di-Pertuan Agung while others are elected by the legislatures of individual states. Members are elected every five years and the current government is a coalition of Barisan National parties with Dato' Seri Abdullah Ahmad Badawi as Prime Minister. State governments are

Above: Indians are a minority race

elected for the same period of office but there is no upper house.

Before the Asian economic meltdown in 1997, Malaysia's GDP growth averaged 8 percent for a decade. The 'Tiger Nation' was well on its way to achieving its goal of developed nation status by 2020. The major shift from agriculture to manufacturing pushed the country into the top 20 largest trading nations in the world. Post-1997, the per annum GDP growth looks set to hover around the 3 percent mark, especially in light of the global and US slowdown. The US is Malaysia's largest trading partner followed by Singapore, Japan and China.

Unemployment remains low although inflation is climbing, and economic resuscitation includes stabilising the ringgit and stimulating both domestic and external demand for Malaysian-produced goods. A key strategy in economic growth is a movement from a pure production economy to a knowledge economy facilitated by information and communications technology.

Malaysia is currently one of the world's largest producers of palm oil, with electrical and electronics products making up more than half its exports. Chemicals, petroleum, machinery, wood products and textiles are its other major products.

How Not to Offend

Shoes should be removed before entering a Malaysian home or place of worship. When in a mosque, visitors who are inappropriately dressed should put on a robe, which will be provided, and cover their limbs. Women should avoid wearing short skirts or shorts and should cover their heads with a scarf.

Pointing with the forefinger, pointing your feet at a person or touching a person's head is considered rude.

MONEY MATTERS

The Malaysian dollar is the ringgit (abbreviated to RM), which is worth 100 sen. Bank notes come in several denominations: RM1 (blue), RM2 (purple), RM5 (green), RM10 (red), RM20 (brownish-orange), RM50 (bluish-green), and RM100 (purple).

Coins come in denominations of RM1 and 50, 20, 10, 5 and 1 sen. Aside from everyday usage, coins are specifically needed for public phones (at 10 sen per local call), driver-operated ticket dispensers in public buses and vending machines for train and monorail tickets.

The ringgit was fixed at RM3.80 to US$ at press time. Due to currency control regulations imposed in 1998, the ringgit can not be traded outside the country.

Money changers can be found all over the city. Although rates vary, they offer better exchange rates than banks.

Traveller's cheques are accepted at major hotels, restaurants and department stores although banks will give you the best rate.

Credit cards such as American Express, Diner's Club, MasterCard and Visa are widely accepted by most establishments throughout Kuala Lumpur. Note that retail shops may impose a 2–5 percent surcharge if you pay for your shopping by credit card.

Tipping

Check if a service charge is added to your bill. You do not have to tip if it is. However whenever good service is rendered, a small tip will be much appreciated. Taxis generally expect the exact meter fare.

GETTING AROUND

Taxis

Kuala Lumpur is well served by a system of highways which bring commuters, taxis, buses and cars into the centre of the city. While traffic jams have not yet reached Bangkok's disastrous gridlocks, they are well on the way.

Kuala Lumpur's taxis are conspicuously painted yellow and black or red and white. They offer a convenient and economical eans of moving around the city, and drivers ually speak at least a smattering of English.

Air-conditioning and fare meters are compulsory in all taxis. Make sure the meter is witched on after you get in. Rates are RM2 r the first 2km (1.24 miles) and 10 sen for ch additional 200m (½ mile). There is a rcharge of RM1 for booking a taxi by one. There is also a 50 percent surcharge the meter fare between midnight and 6am. there are more than two passengers per i, 20 sen per additional passenger is levied.

City taxis cannot legally pick passengers at the airport *(see page 80)* where a upon system is in use but you can take a ty taxi to the airport.

It is fairly easy to get a taxi either by eueing at taxi stands, flagging one down the street, or booking one by telephone. y to avoid hailing one between 3pm and 30pm, as taxi drivers change shifts around is time and usually do not pick up passengers unless you are going their way. Note: will also be difficult to get a taxi in heavy jammed areas during rush hours.

Half- and full-day taxi charters to places the Klang Valley *(all City Itineraries and xcursions 1, 3 & 4)* range from RM20 – 5 per hour, excluding toll charges. You can so book with reliable taxi companies such **Comfort** (tel: 03-8024 2727) and **New upercab** (tel: 03-7875 7333); call at least ur hours beforehand.

Buses

here are several companies providing bus ansportation services in Kuala Lumpur. hey include **Rapid KL**, **Len Seng** and **ark May** (air-conditioned). Air-con buses re 50 sen upwards.

The main inner city bus stops are Puduaya, the Klang Bus Station near Chinatown, angkok Bank behind Central Market, ebuh Ampang, and the Jalan Tuanku Abul Rahman/Jalan Ipoh intersection in Chow it. Buses can be packed like sardine cans uring peak periods, so watch your wallets.

Rental Cars

or seeing the city in style, opt for a chauffered limousine offered by a number of local car-rental companies, includng **Avis**, **udget**, **Hertz** and **National**. Most hotels also provide air-conditioned limo services, but they tend to be more expensive.

For self-drive cars, rental rates vary according to insurance options and vehicle type, but rates generally start at RM150 per day.

Train and Light Rail

KTM Berhad also administers the Rawang to Klang **KTM Komuter** electrified commuter rail service, which transports commuters and travellers within greater Kuala Lumpur and the Klang Valley.

Within the city, the **Light Rail Transport** (LRT) is an integrated monorail system operated by two concessionaires, Putra and Star. Air-conditioned and very convenient, the LRT services areas such as Jalan Ampang, Chow Kit, Petaling Jaya and Bangsar. Feeder buses go to suburbs and shopping centres. Ask for maps at any LRT station. The **Monorail** covers the Bukit Bintang, Kampung Bahru, Chow Kit and Titiwangsa areas.

The central hub for all these services is the modern **Stesen Sentral Kuala Lumpur** (tel: 03-2279 8888; www.stesensentral.com); here you can also catch the KLIA Express to the airport.

Maps

Tourism Malaysia (tel: 03-2615 8188) has free maps and guides from its information counters *(see page 90)* and in most hotels. The maps show routes, landmarks and commuter train and LRT stops within the city.

You can also get maps and more information from the **Malaysia Tourism Centre** (MTC) *(see page 90)*. City tours can be booked here too, as well as tours to places like Taman Negara and Pulau Langkawi.

HOURS & HOLIDAYS

Business Hours

Business hours are from 8.30am or 9am to 5pm, Monday to Friday. Many businesses are also open on Saturday from 8.30 or 9am, closing by 12.30pm or 1pm. Government offices are open Monday to Friday 8am–4.15pm, and Saturday 8am–12.45pm. There is a long lunch break on Friday from 12.45pm to 2.45pm for Friday Muslim prayers.

Banks are open Monday to Friday 10am–3pm, and Saturday 9.30am–11.30pm. Post offices open Monday to Saturday 8am–4.30pm, while a handful in large housing estates are open until 10pm. The General Post Office at Menara Dayabumi, Jalan Sultan Hishamuddin, has longer opening hours. The first and third Saturday of the month is a government and banking off-day. Hotels will mail letters and sell stamps at the reception desk. Almost all department stores, supermarkets and shopping complexes are open daily from 10am to 10pm. Otherwise, shops close earlier, between 6.30–7.30pm and on Sunday.

Public Holidays

Following are official public holidays in Kuala Lumpur. Dates of ethnic festivals vary; they are determined by various lunar calendars. Check precise dates with Tourism Malaysia:

New Year's Day: January 1
Federal Territory Day: February 1
Chinese New Year: January/February
Hari Raya Puasa: Date varies
Labour Day: May 1
Wesak Day: May/June
HM the King's Birthday: June 5
Hari Raya Haji: Date varies
National Day: August 31
Prophet Muhammad's Birthday: Date varies
Deepavali: October/November
Christmas Day: December 25

ACCOMMODATION

Hotels

There is a glut of hotel rooms, which means that quality accommodation is more than affordable. Do not hesitate to negotiate for better rates than what is quoted. Hotels are all air-conditioned and complemented by restaurants and bars. Five-star hotels have swimming pools, fitness centres, shops and other facilities. Rack rates for standard double rooms are divided into five price ranges:

$ = below RM100
$$ = RM100–199
$$$ = RM200–299
$$$$ = RM300–399
$$$$$ = above RM400

Carcosa Seri Negara
Taman Tasik Perdana
Tel: 03-2282 1888; Fax: 03-2282 7888
www.carcosa.com.my
Immaculate all-suite hotel housed in former Governor-General's residence and s in a private park. Its 13 suites come wi private butler service. $$$$$

Mandarin Oriental
Kuala Lumpur City Centre
Tel: 03-2380 8888; Fax: 03-380-8833
www.mandarinoriental.com
Luxury accommodations, with marble bath rooms, next to the world's tallest building Pricier rooms have great views of the Twi Towers. Just next door is shopping galor at the mega-sized Suria KLCC Mall. $$$$$

The Regent
160 Jalan Bukit Bintang
Tel: 03-2141 8000; Fax: 03-2142 1441
www.regenthotels.com
A polished establishment with elegant room excellent service and restaurants. Its hip Ogg Italian restaurant is highly recommended fc a great night out. Conveniently located fc shopping at the fringe of Bukit Bintang. $$$$

Shangri-La
11 Jalan Sultan Ismail
Tel: 03-2032 2388; Fax: 03-2032 1514
www.shangri-la.com
Stylish hotel that is centrally located in th business district and famed for its cuisine Recent renovations have turned this into on of the best addresses in the city. $$$$$

Grand Plaza Parkroyal
54 Jalan Sultan Ismail
Tel: 03-2142 5588; Fax: 03-2141 4281
www.parkroyalhotels.com
A well-located property in the heart of the Bukit Bintang shopping district. $$$$

JW Marriott
Star Hill Centre, 181 Jalan Bukit Bintang
Tel: 03-2715 9000; Fax: 03-2715 7000
www.marriott.com
An upmarket and stylish hotel, close to al the major shopping centres at Buki Bintang. Its award-winning restaurant, Thir Floor, is popular with KL's gourmets. $$$$$

practical information

...enaissance
...r Jalan Sultan Ismail/Jalan Ampang
l: 03-2162 2233/6888; Fax: 03-2163 1122
...w.renaissance-kul.com
...uropean-themed business hotel at the tip
...the Golden Triangle. Ask for rooms that
...ve you great views of the Petronas Twin
...wers. $$$$

...oncorde
Jalan Sultan Ismail
l: 03-2144 2200; Fax: 03-2144 1628
...vw.concorde.net/kl
...ot far from the shopping district and close
...trendy restaurants and nightlife spots. Its
...ore expensive Premier wing has nicer
...oms and a separate check-in facility. Also
...uses the popular Hard Rock Café. $$$

...rown Princess
...lan Tun Razak
...l: 03-2162 5522; Fax: 03-2162 4687
...ww.crownprincess.com.my
...well-appointed hotel, located next to sev-
...al big shopping malls. Over 500 rooms
...d an award-winning Indian restaurant. $$$

...rowne Plaza Mutiara KL
...lan Sultan Ismail
...l: 03-2148 2322; Fax: 03-2144 2157
...ww.crowneplaza.com
...art of a local chain and extensively reno-
...ated, this hotel is a short walk away from
...e KLCC, Golden Triangle and Bukit Bin-
...ng areas. $$$

...otel Equatorial
...lan Sultan Ismail
...l: 03-2161 7777; Fax: 03-2161 7920
...ww.equatorial.com
...n international-class hotel located midway
...etween the KLCC area and Bukit Bintang.
...a stone's throw away is the Jalan Sultan
...smail entertainment district. $$$

...ederal
...5 Jalan Bukit Bintang
...l: 03-2148 9166; Fax: 03-2148 2877
...ww.federal.com.my
...ne of Kuala Lumpur's first hotels in the
...eart of Bukit Bintang but still well main-
...ained. Good value for money. It has a well-
...nown revolving restaurant. $$$

Hotel Grand Maya
Jalan Ampang
Tel: 03-2711 8866; Fax: 03-2711 8601
www.grandmaya.com.my
Formerly the Park Plaza, the rather forbid-
ding glass and steel façade belies its more
gracious interior. Serves a mainly business
clientele. $$$

Hotel Istana
Jalan Raja Chulan
Tel: 03-2141 9988; Fax: 03-2144 0111
www.meritus-hotels.com
A 516-room hotel, centrally located to business and shops. Good Italian restaurant and
a bar overlooking a landscaped garden. $$$

The Legend Hotel
Jalan Putra
Tel: 03-4042 9888; Fax: 03-4043 0700
www.legendsgroup.com/legendkl
Part of the Legend chain of hotels in Malaysia.
Ideally located next to The Mall and opposite
the Putra World Trade Centre. $$$

Meliá Kuala Lumpur
16 Jalan Imbi
Tel: 03-2142 8333; Fax: 03-2142 6623
www.solmelia.com
Recently refurbished quality accommodations only a short distance from the enter-
tainment hub of Bukit Bintang. $$$

Right: plush Shangri-La Hotel

Pan Pacific
Jalan Putra
Tel: 03-4042 5555; Fax: 03-4043 8717
www.panpac.com
Starting to show its age but with a good location, this hotel is situated near the Putra World Trade Centre and The Mall north of the city centre. Ride the glass elevator perched outside the building for grand views of the city. $$$

AnCasa
(formerly Impiana Hotel Kuala Lumpur)
Jalan Tun Tan Cheng Lock
Tel: 03-2026 6060; Fax: 03-2031 3350
Next to the frenetic Puduraya Bus Station, with Chinatown on its other side. Perfect for spending the night if you have an early morning bus to catch. $$

Fortuna
87 Jalan Berangan
Tel: 03-2141 9111; Fax: 03-2141 8237
e-mail: fortuna@po.jaring.my
Small but central; in a quiet area behind the main Bukit Bintang area. $$

Hotel Grand Continental
Jalan Raja Laut
Tel: 03-2693 9333; Fax: 03-2693 9732
www.grandhotelsinternational.com
Located near the Jalan Tuanku Abdul Rahman shopping area. Rooms are a tacky shade of pink so beware. $$

Mandarin Pacific
2 Jalan Sultan
Tel: 03-2070 3000; Fax: 03-2070 4363
e-mail: mandpac@tm.net.my
Also in the heart of Chinatown, close to major bus and taxi terminals and the Central Market cultural centre. $$

Swiss Inn
62 Jalan Sultan
Tel: 03-2072 3333; Fax: 03-2013 6699
www.swissgarden.com
This is a popular hotel located in the heart of Chinatown. Styled after the Malaya of the 1900s, the rooms are small but comfortable, and you feel like you are right in the thick of the never-sleeping Chinatown action. $$

Grand Paradise Masjid India
62 Jalan Masjid India
Tel: 03-2693 0144; Fax: 03-2693 2422
In the heart of Little India and surrounded excellent shopping, though entertainme options are limited. $

Youth Hostels
KL International Youth Hostel
21 Jalan Kampung Attap
Tel: 03-2273 6870; Fax: 03-2274 1115
Budget accommodations situated with walking distance of Chinatown and maj bus terminals. $

YMCA
95 Jalan Padang, Brickfields
Tel: 03-2274 1439; Fax: 03-2274 0559
Near the town centre, easily accessible b public transport. $

Guest Houses
Many small hotels housed above shop uni can be found in the city, especially alon Jalan Tuanku Abdul Rahman and in th Chow Kit and Bukit Bintang areas. Bette known by their Malay name, *rumah tumpar gan* (lodging houses), some of them are qui reputable. For example, the Merdeka Hote in Jalan Raja Muda offers decent rooms a low prices; rates range from RM40–55.

HEALTH & EMERGENCIES
Hygiene
Drink only boiled water and bottled c canned drinks. If you have a very sensitiv stomach, avoid ice cubes, especially i streetside stalls and small coffeeshops, a the ice cubes here are usually made usin unboiled water. Restaurants and other eatin places offer boiled water. Mineral and bo tled water is widely available everywher and is reasonably priced. Food served in li censed restaurants and at hawker stalls i mostly clean. Regular customers are ver important for hawker stalls so most try an keep their stalls and utensils clean.

Pharmacies are found in most shoppin complexes. They are well-stocked and hav registered pharmacists. Controlled drugs ar sold only by prescription.

ospitals

any hotels have doctors on call to treat ergencies. Kuala Lumpur has a number hospitals offering good medical care. Both vernment and private hospitals have fully-uipped emergency and intensive care units cope with any medical crisis.

The **General Hospital** is at Jalan Pahang, : 03-2692 1044, and the **Universiti Hos-al** is at Jalan Universiti in suburban Petal-g Jaya; its emergency ward can be ntacted at tel: 03-7956 4422 ext 2501. ey are both government-owned hospitals.

Private hospitals include: **Tawakal Spe-alist Centre**, 202-A Jalan Pahang, tel: 03-23 3599; CMH **Medical Centre**, 106 Jalan du, tel: 03-2078 2055; **Pantai Medical entre**, 8 Jalan Bukit Pantai, tel: 03-2296 88; **Subang Jaya Medical Centre**, 1 Jalan 12/1A Subang Jaya, tel: 03-5634 1212.

ledical and Dental Clinics

here are many 24-hour polyclinics, and ivately-owned specialist clinics, which fer treatment in the city. Registered med-al practitioners and qualified dental sur-ons are listed in the Yellow Pages of the lephone directory.

olice Emergencies

all **999** for police and ambulance services; d **994** for fire and rescue emergencies.

mergency Repairs

avement cobblers and key grinders are und on almost every other downtown street d in shopping complexes. They do a pretty od job at fairly low prices. Some of them so make rubber stamps and signs.

COMMUNICATIONS & NEWS

elecommunications

elephone, telegram, mail, telex and fax cilities are offered by most hotels, and the case of medium-budget to luxury tels, IDD (international direct dial) phones e available in guest rooms. To call abroad rectly, first dial the international access de 00, followed by the country code: ustralia (61); France (33); Germany (49);

Italy (39); Japan (81); Netherlands (31); Spain (34); UK (441); US and Canada (1).

To call Kuala Lumpur from overseas, dial the international country code 60 for Malaysia, followed by 3, the area code for Kuala Lumpur.

International calls can be made at any **Kedai Telekom** (Telecoms shops) located in the city during office hours. A 24-hour service is available at the **Central Telekom Building** in Jalan Raja Chulan. IDD pay phones are also available in popular loca-tions. They accept most major credit cards.

The cost of a local call through a public payphone is 10 sen. Payphones maintained at shops and restaurants charge twice or three times that amount. Calls may also be made using pre-paid phone cards. These cards, sold in denominations of RM5–RM100, are very convenient and can be purchased at selected stores such as 7-Eleven and news-stands. Payphones using these phone cards are usu-ally in better working order since they are less prone to vandalism.

Note, however, that payphones are main-tained by three companies, Uniphone, Citi-phone and Telekom Malaysia, and that the various phone cards are not interchangeable.

Internet cafés are found everywhere, par-ticularly in shopping centres, and charges range from RM4–10 per hour.

Shipping

Larger shops will handle documentation and shipping for purchases, or will recommend handling agents to do the job.

Stationery shops and some post offices sell boxes for goods to be sent by mail.

ight: a public telephone booth

News Media

There are several English dailies in Peninsular Malaysia: *The Star* and *The Sun* (morning tabloids), *The New Straits Times* (morning broadsheet) and *Malay Mail* (afternoon tabloid). The two largest selling newspapers, *The Star* and *The New Straits Times*, offer comprehensive coverage of both local and foreign news. Business coverage is covered by *The Edge* weekly. The *Asian Wall Street Journal, International Herald Tribune* and *USA Today* can be obtained at most newsstands and bookshops. Leading international periodicals and magazines are available at large bookshops and hotel news sellers.

Cable TV is available in most hotels, including CNN, CNBC and HBO. The specialist hotel programme packager is Vision 4. Free-to-air local TV stations are those run by state-owned Radio Televisyen Malaysia (RTM), and private stations TV3, NTV7, 8TV and Channel 9. All air local news reports, including in English, and mainstream American mini-series and comedies alongside religious Islamic programmes.

Radio Music KL is a special 24-hour service for Kuala Lumpur and has programmes for visitors and travellers. It is broadcast by RTM on 97.2 MHz. FM radio has a range of English-language musical programmes from classical and jazz to pop. RTM also broadcasts an English service, Radio Four Network, between 6am and 12am. English-language news bulletins are broadcast hourly. Flip through the stations and you will be able to hear everything, ranging from canto-pop and Hindi movie film hits to Malay rock tunes.

SPORTS

Swimming

Almost all hotels charging RM200 a above have swimming pools.

Public pools at **Bangsar Sports Comple** (tel: 03-2284 6065); **Chin Woo Stadium** (t 03-2072 4602); **Club Syabas** (tel: 03-79. 3322) are open from 9am to 9pm.

In addition, there is a massive water ther park in Bandar Sunway called the **Sunwa Lagoon** (tel: 03-5635 6000). See Itinera 11 *(page 50)* for more details.

Jogging

Taman Tasik Perdana (Lake Gardens **Taman Tasik Titiwangsa** off Jalan T Razak, **Taman Tasik Permaisuri** in Chera **Taman Tunku Abdul Rahman**, and t **KLCC Park** have jogging paths.

Gym and Fitness Centres

Many hotels have fully-equipped fitness ce tres or gyms. Also try the Weld, Wisma SP PJ Hilton and Mid Valley Megamall.

Court and Racquet Games

Sports complexes in and around the ci offer facilities for badminton, tennis, squas volleyball, table tennis and *sepak takraw* (local ball game). Courts are open from 7a or 8am till 11pm or midnight: **Bangsa Sports Complex** (tel: 03-2284 6065 **Dewan Datuk Keramat** (tel: 03-425 4863); **Taman Tasik Titiwangsa** (tel: 0. 4025 2063); and **National Sports Counc Complex** (tel: 03-8992 9600).

Bowling

Bowling alleys can be found at: **Feder Hotel**, Jalan Bukit Bintang, **Wisma Miram** on the 5th floor, **Yow Chuan Plaza**, Jala Tun Razak, and the **Sunway Pyramic** where the national bowling team trains.

Golf

Malaysia is often called a golfer's paradis There are literally hundreds of golf course in the country, some of them designed b luminaries like Ronald Fream, Jack Nicklau and Robert Trent Jones Jr. There are ove 50 courses alone within an easy hour's driv from Kuala Lumpur. Some of these course

Above: Malaysia is often called a golfer's paradise

so offer night golfing under floodlights.

Close to the city is the **Saujana Golf and Country Club** (tel: 03-7846 1466) located near the Subang Airport, with a 36-hole golf course. Other clubs in the vicinity include the **Sultan Abdul Aziz Shah Golf Club** (tel: 03-5510 5872), **Glenmarie Golf and Country Club** (tel: 03-7803 9090), both in Shah Alam. The Sultan Abdul Aziz Shah also offers facilities for night golfing.

Further from KL is the **Rahman Putra Golf and Country Club** in Sungai Buluh (tel: 03-6156 6870); **Templer Golf and Country Club** in Rawang (tel: 03-6091 5517); **Awana Golf Club** in Genting Highlands (tel: 03-6101 3015); and **Sri Morib Golf Club** (tel: 03-3198 1418).

Most clubs charge green fees for non-members. Further details may be obtained from the Malaysian Golf Association, situated at 14 Jalan 4/7C, tel: 03-9283 7300, www.mgaonline.com.my.

LANGUAGE

The Malay language, or Bahasa Malaysia, is polysyllabic, with variations in syllables to convey changes in meaning, unlike tonal languages such as Mandarin, Cantonese or Thai. For example, *duduk* (sit) is a verb. By adding the prefix *ke* and suffix *an*, we get the noun *kedudukan*, which means position. By adding a different prefix, *pen*, we get another noun, *penduduk*, which means inhabitant. Adding an *i* after *duduk* turns it into an active verb (to sit), while *menduduki* is a present continuous verb.

Tones do not vary to give different meanings and, for the most part, words are pronounced as they are spelt. In general, the pronunciation is the same as in English, with a few exceptions. In Bahasa Malaysia, 'a' is pronounced 'ar' as in tar. The letter 'e' has an 'er' sound, as in reserve. You will also find that 'c' is pronounced 'ch' as in chair; the letter 'g' is always hard, as in gun and garden, not as in ginger; and 'sy' is pronounced 'sh'.

The language uses two distinct scripts: *Jawi* and *Rumi. Jawi* is the Arabic form of writing; *Rumi* the Roman alphabet, considered the easier of the two and also the official script of the country.

Here is a small vocabulary list to get you on your way.

Numbers

1	*Satu*
2	*Dua*
3	*Tiga*
4	*Empat*
5	*Lima*
6	*Enam*
7	*Tujuh*
8	*Lapan*
9	*Sembilan*
10	*Sepuluh*
11	*Sebelas*
12	*Dua belas*
13	*Tiga belas*
20	*Dua puluh*
21	*Dua puluh satu*
100	*Seratus*
1,000	*Seribu*

Greetings and Others

How do you do?	*Apa khabar?*
Good morning	*Selamat pagi*
Good afternoon	*Selamat petang*
Good evening	*Selamat malam*
Goodbye	*Selamat tinggal*
Bon voyage	*Selamat jalan*
Fine/good	*Baik*
Thank you	*Terima kasih*
Please	*Tolong/sila*
Excuse me	*Maafkan saya*
I am sorry	*Saya minta maaf*
You're welcome	*Sama-sama*
What is your name?	*Siapa nama anda?*
My name is...	*Nama saya...*
Please be careful	*Berhati-hati*
Yes	*Ya*
No	*Tidak*

Pronouns

I	*Saya*
You	*Anda/awak*
He/she	*Dia*
We	*Kami*
They	*Mereka*

Forms of Address

Mr	*Encik*
Mrs	*Puan*
Miss	*Cik*

practical information

Directions and Travel

Where	*Di mana*
Right	*Kanan*
Left	*Kiri*
Turn	*Belok*
Go	*Pergi*
Stop	*Berhenti*
Follow	*Ikut*
Near	*Dekat*
Far	*Jauh*
Inside	*Dalam*
Outside	*Luar*
Front	*Hadapan*
Behind	*Belakang*
Here	*Sini*
There	*Sana*
Road	*Jalan*
Street	*Jalan*
Lane	*Lorong*
Bridge	*Jambatan*
Junction	*Simpang*
North	*Utara*
South	*Selatan*
East	*Timur*
West	*Barat*

Useful Phrases

How much?	*Berapa harganya?*
Can you help me?	*Bolehkah encik tolong saya?*
Where is this place?	*Di mana tempat ini?*
How far?	*Berapa jauh?*
I want to go to…	*Saya hendak pergi ke…*
Stop here	*Tolong berhenti sini*
Expensive	*Mahal*
Lower the price	*Kurangkan harganya*
Too big	*Besar sangat*
Too small	*Kecil sangat*
Any other colour?	*Ada warna lain?*

Other Handy Words

Drink	*Minum* (verb), *Minuman* (noun)
Eat	*Makan* (verb), *Makanan* (noun)
Fruit	*Buah-buahan*
Water	*Air*
Have	*Ada*
Don't have	*Tidak ada*
Toilet	*Tandas*
Why?	*Mengapa?*

When?	*Bila?*
Hot (spicy)	*Pedas*
Hot (heat)	*Panas*
Cold	*Sejuk*
Sweet	*Manis*
Sour	*Masam*
Delicious	*Sedap*
Clean	*Bersih*
Dirty	*Kotor*
Beautiful	*Cantik*
Open	*Buka*
Close	*Tutup*
Never	*Tidak pernah*
Often	*Selalu*
Sometimes	*Kadang-kadang*

USEFUL ADDRESSES

Tourist Offices

Tourism Malaysia
Level 2, 24–27th and 30th floor
Putra World Trade Centre, Jalan Tun Isma
Tel: 03-2615 8188; fax: 03-2693 0207
e-mail: *tourism@tourism.gov.my*
www.tourismmalaysia.gov.my
Its information-filled website has a list c
all public holidays and major events. Touris
Malaysia information centres are also foun
at the following locations: KL Sentral, te
03-2272 5823; and KLIA (arrival hall), te
03-8776 5651.

Malaysia Tourism Centre (MTC)
109, Jalan Ampang
Tel: 03-2164 3929 (open 7am–midnight)
The staff are knowledgeable and very help
ful with tourist enquiries.

Travel Agents

Asian Overland Services Tours and Trave
No. 39C&40C, Jalan Mamanda 9,
Ampang Point
Tel: 03-4252 9100; fax: 03-4252 9800
e-mail: *aos@asian overland.com.my*
www.asianoverland.com
Reliable agency offering KL city tours a
well as adventure and ecotourism package
outside of KL and the rest of Malaysia.

Tour 51
1st flr, Wisma Centre, 176 Jalan Ampang
Tel: 03-2161 8830; fax: 03-2162 2837

Right: window watchers

mail: cytan51@pd.jaring.my
tablished company with a good reputa-
·n and knowledgeable guides.

·alaysia Travel Business
rC, 109 Jalan Ampang
l: 03-2163 0162; fax: 03-2162 9439
mail: chris@mtbiz.com.my
ffices in the MTC and major hotels; tours
·n be organised for a minimum of 2 people.

FURTHER READING

·ooks are expensive in Malaysia and selec-
·ns are generally not very good, the most
·mprehensive being Kinokuniya in Suria
·LCC. Every mall is bound to have at least
·ıe outlet of these bookshop chains: Times,
·PH, or Popular (mainly Chinese books).
·rt books can be purchased from Page One
· Lot 10 and the Islamic Arts Museum shop,
·hilst good selections of second-hand books
·ın be found at Skoob in Petaling Jaya.

Adoi, by Lee Kit, Times Books Intl, Sin-
·ıpore/Kuala Lumpur, 1989. A humourous,
·ell-illustrated satire of Malaysian foibles.

Beaches of Malaysia, The Department of
·rigation and Drainage, Malaysia and De-
·gn Dimension Sdn Bhd, 1997. The first
·mprehensive photographic record of more
·ıan 168 beaches in Malaysia.

Chinatown, Kuala Lumpur, by Steve
·ristow, and Edwin Lee, Tropical Press,
·uala Lumpur, 1994. Excellent photographs
·ıd history of Chinatown.

Culture Shock! Malaysia and Singapore,
·y Jo-Ann Craig, Times Books Intl. Inter-
·sting notes on the country's customs.

Insight Guide Malaysia, Apa Publica-
·ons, Singapore, 2001. Best-selling book
·ːtains the basic structure of the original
·ɔok published in 1985, with scores of new
·hotographs and updated text.

Kuala Lumpur – A Sketchbook, by Chin
·on Yit and Chen Voon Fee, Archipelago
·ress, Singapore, 1998. Beautiful water-
·ɔlour paintings of old Kuala Lumpur with
·ıitably brief captions.

Maugham's Malaysian Stories, by Som-
·rset Maugham, 1993, reprinted 1986. Mas-
·rful story-telling of British colonial life.

The Crafts of Malaysia, Dato' Haji Sulaiman Othman, Yeoh Jin Leng, etc,
Archipelago Press, Singapore, 1994. A beautiful documentary of the development of the
Malay arts in a changing society, with pic-
tures of the best craft from museums.

The Food of Malaysia, edited by Wendy
Hutton, Periplus Editions, Singapore, 1995.
Handy-sized collection of local recipes with
useful background information and lovely
colour photographs.

The Malayan Trilogy, by Anthony
Burgess, Penguin Books, London. Burgess'
famous novel on post-war Malaya during
the chaotic upheaval of independence.

The Malay Archipelago, by Alfred Rus-
sel Wallace, Graham Brash, Singapore,
1987. Wallace's famous account of his travels in the region.

The Malays – A Cultural History, by
Richard Winstedt, revised and updated by
Tham Seong Chee, Graham Brash, Singapore, 1981. A fascinating documentation of
the Malays from pre-history to present day.

The Malay Dilemma Revisited, by M
Bakri Musa, To Excel Inc, 1999. A glimpse
of Malaysia's preferential race policy and its
impact on social and economic dynamics.
The book title is a take on the original *The
Malay Dilemma,* written by ex-Prime Minister Mahathir Mohamad when he was ex-
iled into political wilderness in 1969.

practical information

INSIGHT
Pocket Guides

Insight Pocket Guides pioneered a new approach to guidebooks, introducing the concept of the authors as "local hosts" who would provide readers with personal recommendations, just as they would give honest advice to a friend who came to stay. They also included a full-size pull-out map.

Now, to cope with the needs of the 21st century, new editions in this growing series are being given a new look to make them more practical to use, and restaurant and hotel listings have been greatly expanded.

☆ INSIGHT GUIDE

The world's largest collection visual travel guides

Now in association with

ACKNOWLEDGEMENTS

Cover	**Jon Arnold/Taxi/Getty Images**
Backcover	**Arthur Teng**
Photography	**Ingo Jezierski/Apa Photo and**
Pages 15T, 25B, 56	**Axiom**
33, 40T, 60, 61, 72, 75	**H. Berbar/HBL**
32, 42, 74	**V. Couarraze/HBL**
62	**Courtesy of The Smokehouse Hotel**
8/9, 50, 87	**Goh Seng Cheng**
10,11	**Mary Evans Picture Library**
5, 6B, 52, 53, 54	**R. Mohd. Noh**
12T	**Muzium Negara, Malaysia**
1, 15B, 28T, 35T/B, 91	**Christine Osborne**
48, 68	**Photobank Singapore**
13	**Picture Library/KL**
12B	**private archives**
14	**Paul Quayle**
2/3, 16, 24	**Chris Stowers/Panos Pictures**
21, 22, 29, 30, 31, 38, 40B, 41, 45, 46, 49, 51, 55, 57, 63, 64, 66, 70, 73, 76, 77, 78, 79, 85	**Arthur Teng**

Cartography	**Berndston & Berndston**
Cover Design	**Carlotta Junger**
Production	**Tanvir Virdee/Caroline Low**

© APA Publications GmbH & Co. Verlag KG Singapore Branch, Singapore

INDEX